# The Daredevil of the Army

# The Daredevil of the Army
A Motorcycle Despatch Rider and 'Buzzer' in the
British Army During the First World War

Austin Patrick Corcoran

LEONAUR

*The Daredevil of the Army*
*A Motorcycle Despatch Rider and 'Buzzer' in the British Army*
*During the First World War*
by Austin Patrick Corcoran

First published under the title
*The Daredevil of the Army*

Leonaur is an imprint of Oakpast Ltd

Copyright in this form © 2011 Oakpast Ltd

ISBN: 978-0-85706-729-6 (hardcover)
ISBN: 978-0-85706-730-2 (softcover)

**http://www.leonaur.com**

Publisher's Notes

# Contents

*Death, capture, accidents—any may overtake him on his road, but none may deter or terrify him. 'The daredevil'—that is the name he earned in the early days of the war, when General French credited him with the salvation of the British forces. And so I introduce him to you, reader—'The Daredevil,' with his coadjutor, equally daring, the 'Buzzer,' the men who supply the 'nerves' and much of the 'Nerve' of the modern fighting army.*

# Foreword

After the manner of a distinguished countryman, I speak my own prologue, not that I may the better explain the action of the coming piece, but rather that I may tell the reason of its being.

"I learned," wrote Sir John French, concerning activities round Mons, "that General Lanrezac was retreating on my right, that at least three German corps were moving against our front and another German corps trying to turn our left wing. Whereupon it was decided to fallback."

"I learned!"

Suppose he had not learned. Suppose, that relying on French support, he had stood at Mons with his 75,000 men and 250 guns to face a victorious army of at least 200,000. Suppose he had defied von Kluck, quite unaware that von Buelow, also victorious, was threatening his flank. Suppose it, and you are supposing the annihilation of the British Army due to the failure of its Motor Cycle Despatch Corps.

"I learned," "information reached me"—the public reads the words every day, never once pausing to consider what they signify. "The news reached me!"

How?

Before the eyes of the initiated rises the picture of the despatch rider, tissue paper strapped to his finger, revolver strapped to his waist, scurrying at his sixty-odd miles an hour over a shell-shot and often enemy-infested highway.

The Motor Cycle Despatch Corps belongs to that branch of the British Service which is known as the Signal Section of the

Royal Engineers. Metaphorically and very happily this branch has been named the "nerves of the modern army." They supply the channels through which the brain of the command communicates its orders to the main body. Block those channels: disconnect the mind from any single member. Immediately that member becomes paralytic, so to speak, unable to move, or at least to make its movements articulate with those of the other members.

Now suppose this huge body extended over a surface of some fifty miles. Suppose it at rest, as we shall see it later in our narrative, when the armies had settled down to the trench deadlock. An elaborate nervous system composed of some thousand of telephone cables, telegraph lines, wireless aerials and the hundred other minor signalling apparatus, keep all its parts in intimate intercommunication. Radiating over the whole line, they all issue from a single point—General Headquarters, the seat of army authority. Where is the fighting most stubborn, the casualties most severe, the supplies most scarce, the men most exhausted? A quivering nerve tells the tale of the strength or weakness of each individual member, and the brain issues its orders accordingly.

A comparatively easy matter is this maintenance of the nervous system when the armies are, comparatively speaking, at rest.,

But put the great body in continuous movement, as it was in the retreat from Mons, or in the advance after the Marne, or in the swift sweep forward from the Somme, or falling back again surely but slowly, as it was in the great spring drive of 1918. Immediately that elaborate system of cable and aerial communication collapses more or less according to the speed of the movement and the effectiveness of enemy fire. Individual effort, of course, is exerted to keep it intact. But it is a shaky system at best, ever on the verge of sudden collapse. And yet now above all times such a system is essential, if the success of the advance or retreat is to be maintained. For if the body advances a foot on one section of the line, while the other foot remains in its old position, at once the stability of the whole body is threatened. Either the first foot must be withdrawn or it must receive adequate support. Else it will be cut off or become paralysed.

"Information reached me," writes French concerning the Battle of the Aisne, "that the enemy had obtained a footing between the First and Second Army Corps and threatened to cut off communications. General Haig was hard pressed and had no reserve in hand. I placed a cavalry division at his disposal, part of which he used skilfully to prolong and secure the left flank of the Guards Brigade. Some heavy fighting ensued which resulted in the enemy being driven back."

That information reached him through a despatch rider. For when an army is in motion or under a fierce barrage or artillery fire, only individual effort will maintain communications, and that is supplied mainly by the Motor Cycle Despatch Corps.

"Deliver your despatch at all costs"—these are the instructions issued to the cyclist.

If he fails through no fault of his own, there are men to take his place. Five to a brigade, nine to a division—there is always an adequate reserve in hand. If he does not return in a stated time, another sets out automatically to cover the same ground that he travelled. If he does return, it is with evidence that he has accomplished his task. There are three little dockets to every message. One the rider leaves at his own headquarters to show he has been sent with the despatch. One he delivers; and a third, signed by the commander to whom he has been sent, he carries back with him, to prove that his duty was duly done. They take no chances of failure in this service.

Death, capture, accidents—any may overtake him on his road, but none may deter or terrify him. "The daredevil"—that is the name he earned in the early days of the war, when General French credited him with the salvation of the British forces.

And so I introduce him to you, reader—"The Daredevil," with his coadjutor, equally daring, the "Buzzer," the men who supply the "nerves," and, to use American slang, much of the "nerve" of the modern fighting army.

11

# The Author Starts for Berlin on a Motor-Cycle, and Finds Himself Presently on the Marne

## 1

We are awaiting our turn to get aboard the *Biscay* which is lying at her berth in Southampton. It is seven in the evening, and we have been riding all day, covering the hundred-odd miles between Chatham and the sea. Our trip has left us dusty and damp with sweat, and our reception is not tending to relieve our discomfort. Lined up beside us some two thousand Tommies are scanning us with the frank criticism of their kind. Our bikes obviously provoke their amusement, and we ourselves their half-tolerant contempt. Occasionally a fragment of their conversation floats towards us, indicative of their general attitude of mind.

"Who the 'ell are them blokes anyway, Nobby?" one regular remarks to another. "Gwine to fight on bikes, be they?"

"Garn," replies Nobby, with his air of superior wisdom, "they ain't goin' to war. They's goin' to a ryce."

"Ryce, me eye. Look at their uniforms." And then evidently for the first time he looks at them closely himself, and surprise replaces the disgust in his tone. "Gawd Awmighty! if they ain't two up! Gwine to ride over the *Kayser*, Sonny?" He puts the question impertinently to the man nearest him.

For answer he receives a silent scowl, and almost voluntarily we all stiffen to attention, only to be reminded somewhat sharply of our own rawness. After all we are but amateurs at his professional game. Only a week ago—it is still but August 17th—we were civilians, with no thought of entering the service. Now, though we wear the King's own coat and two corporal's stripes adorn our sleeves, we can scarcely claim the title of soldiers. Rigid and severe, we are striving to hide our discouragement under an air of indifference, when suddenly the voice of the sergeant major comes booming across the dock.

"Now will you, gentlemen," a pause on the appellation emphasises its intended sarcasm, "kindly try to get those bikes of yours aboard?"

Instantly a shout goes up from the assembled regiment—the sergeant major has excellent lungs—and amid general jeering we approach the gangplank.

"Rotten blighters! "I hear a mutter in front of me.

So we, the first civilians to take part in the great war, leave England for France and the front. At seven-thirty, after much shouting and shrill screeching of whistles, we finally get under way. My motor-cycle stowed safely in the after-well-deck, I seek a quiet corner outside the Marconi cabin on the hurricane deck, and squatting on a coil of rope, settle myself to think. It is my first time in ten days to indulge in such exercise. All round me is a buzz of conversation. I can hear the clank of an occasional mess tin, as some well-seasoned regular proceeds to make himself at home. Looking about, I see some dozen of his kind, coats open at the collar, belt unloosened, sprawling on benches or on the floor. And the sight of them makes me horribly homesick.

"You're a hot-headed idiot," I decide to myself, "always rushing to the rescue before you know the house is afire." And I heartily wish myself back in the cool grove of Corrientes.

For it was at Barcelona that the first mutterings of the storm found me. Austria and Serbia on the brink of war! The Balkans did not interest me. Russia coming to the rescue! I got a letter from home—there was chance of our being caught in the whirlwind. Hot on the heels of this came the news that Germany was mobilising and France preparing for her own defence. I crossed to England just in time to hear the first cry for volunteers. Then it seemed to come as the answer to a prayer.

If there was any form of adventure which life had still to offer me, I did not know it at the time. I had hunted in the heart of Africa, had ranched in Bolivia; had sailed twice round the earth and seen all its civilisations. But still I was only twenty-six and not yet surfeited with errantry. What next?

War! The greatest of all adventures! I had not thought to find it in my time.

It was in such spirit that I joined the army. No band played me into a recruiting office. No call of patriotism stirred my heart or conscience. I know I am only confessing my own sins, but on my head be they! Just one consideration gave me pause for a moment—again I reveal my lack of grace. I know something of discipline in the navy. I surmised it might be similar in the army, and I had no desire to experience its tedium. To get to France without the dull preliminary drilling of a camp—that was my only object. And when the special call came for University men to form a corps of motor-cycle despatch riders, I fought my way to the recruiting office like the rest.

It was quick work. I passed the doctor, proved myself competent to handle a bike, went to Chatham to get my equipment, and now—here I am, rigged out in His Majesty's regimentals, jeered at by his soldiers, looked askance at by his officers, a "blooming civilian butting in on a soldier's business."

"Lonely, old chap?" I feel a hand on my shoulder, and look up into a pair of grey Scotch eyes. "My name's Grant." He holds out his hand. I take it, and so meet my best friend.

A Dundee lawyer, about my own age, he has joined for more serious considerations. Something of a student, he saw a crisis was coming. Something of a sportsman he wanted to be in the thick of it. So he handed his business over to a *locum tenens*, a man too old to serve, and hurried up to London to join.

For a while we talk on general topics, then on that nearest our hearts. Can we, undisciplined, hastily picked men, really stand the shock of a battle? Is a soldier's business just a matter of nerve, or does it require training? The powers-that-be have frankly acknowledged they are trying an experiment in thus choosing us. The military men have scoffed at their confidence. Are we to set a precedent in favour of individual initiative or are we merely to be horrible examples?

It is ten o'clock before we realise that it is time we have food. But where to get it? Our equipment does not include it.

"Just a tick," says Grant, and leaves me for a moment, to return with a package of sandwiches that he had carefully stowed away into the tool bag of his machine.

Those finished, we nose round in search for more secluded corners. We want to sleep, and we have not yet learned to do it gregariously. Finally we decided in favour of one of the boats that has been turned in. Down we throw ourselves on the cover, thanking heaven we have learned to "rough it." That ride has insured us against the risks of insomnia.

## 2

Dawn wakes us to a raucous sound of snoring and a distant vision of the French coast, on which Havre stands out, a black dot on the dim grey line. It is Grant who rouses me to full consciousness.

"Come on! Let's look for a wash!" I follow him sleepily. We trudge the ship over thoroughly, upper deck, lower deck, middle deck, all the other decks, but no sign of water can we see nor do we meet others bent on a like quest. We have decided that bathing is a luxury not allowed to soldiers and are proceeding to return to our nook when a sudden turn brings us up sharply against a spruce, shining major whom we learn to be the second-in-command of the battalion on board. We have saluted in our self-conscious, rookie fashion and are passing, when he halts us with a raised hand. We stop and are thus ensnared into our first lesson in the nice etiquette of the army.

"Corporal!"

"Yes, sir." Grant is the spokesman.

"What are all you people with bikes doing aboard?"

Grant informs him we are the motor-cycle despatch corps.

"Despatch riders? Why, I had no idea there were so many in the British army. How long have you two been in?"

"Five days, sir."

The major whistles, then looks us quizzically over.

"Five days, and you're going straight into the fun? Rather risky, eh?"

We shrug our shoulders, and he turns to go, when Grant brings him up abruptly with a query. Did he know where we could manage to get a wash? The enormity of the crime in a corporal's thus addressing a major on matters of personal cleanliness hardly comes home to us even after his lecture. We are rather hot under the collar when he finishes his harangue, though he delivers it with all possible consideration. But his next move more than makes up for the humiliation, for he takes us to his own room for a regular wash! He was a thoroughly decent sort, that major!

By the time we have finished, everyone is awake, and the ship is tying up alongside the wharf. All around is a din calculated to deafen tender ears, the clang of accoutrements being adjusted, mess tins, rifles, bayonets—and then the mad cheering of the people on the dock.

Half the civilian population of France, or so it seems to me, must have had word that "*les Anglais*" were arriving. They have gathered there with flags, food, tobacco. Though it pleases us, still their excitement makes us sheepish. What a fearfully demonstrative people they are! We haven't yet realised the imminence of their peril, and their sense of safety in being backed by the British fleet.

It is an hour before the *Biscay* has disgorged her men and cargo. A young officer meets us on the dock, and lines us up away on the right, telling us to await further orders. Meantime our critics, the Tommies, have drawn up in company formation. Soon they are ready for their road—where it leads heaven only knows. Just as they receive the order "Quick March!" there comes an Irish voice, bellowing from the bridge of the boat we are leaving behind.

"So long, Mike!"

A man in the ranks looks back, and waves.

"So long, Tim. It's a long way to Tipperary!" he shouts.

Instantly a laugh goes up from the troop, and a rollicking voice starts the song.

"It's a long wa-ay to Tipperary——"

Soon the whole company has taken it up, and so for the first time of many hundred in France, I see our men swing off to battle to the air of the popular tune.

A strange sense of desolation sweeps over me as I watch them go. Somehow their jaunty air of recklessness brings home to me for the first time the grim reality of the enterprise I am embarked on. I glance at the men beside me, lined up so quietly with their bikes.

Perhaps I am only seeing through the haze of my own feelings, but they, too, strike me as strangely silent and subdued. But we get no time to indulge our desolation, for no sooner has the dock cleared of the Tommies than our officer presents himself again.

"You will ride to Rouen and report there to the Transportation Officer who will direct you to your different sections." His voice is very formal at first, then changes abruptly to a more cheery note. "Off with you!" he orders.

Then, as I am proceeding to mount—I happen to be at the head of the line—he hands me an envelope to be delivered to the T. O. I learned later that it contained a note identifying us.

We are half way across the dock, when a happy thought strikes him.

"*Café* to your right as you go out!" he hollers.

We hear him. We would have heard if we had been miles off. We make for it with all the haste of the really hungry, and, as I eat my omelette and drink my *café au lait*, I have my first opportunity to size up *en masse* the men who are henceforth to be my companions.

3

An English poet, commemorating the early deeds of the despatch rider, named him perhaps appropriately the "daredevil." A less enthusiastic gentleman, describing him since, has called him a "glorified messenger-boy." As a matter of fact, he may be either one or both, according to the character of the fighting. In trench warfare he is more liable to be the latter, but there were no trenches when we went to France.

The duty of a despatch rider,[1] as everyone knows, is to carry confidential messages of urgent importance from one staff officer to another. They may be from a general to a general; they may be merely from a colonel to a captain. Always they are from one commissioned man to another. Which is the reason why he wears a corporal's stripes. According to the regulations of the British army, no man in the ranks may approach such an officer of his own accord, unless accompanied by a non-com. And non-coms are, naturally, of too much importance to be spared as permanent escorts. Were it not for this detail of army etiquette, the despatch rider would be no more than a mere private.

As to the method of performing his duty, there is no definite rule. When we received our instructions in London, they were practically summed up in the following sentence:

"Deliver your despatch as quickly as you can, and then return to your own section."

The how and the when, we were informed, would be matters for our own discretion, and much discretion we needed at times.

Suppose a despatch rider meets with an accident on the road, and his bike is put entirely out of commission. Unseen and unsuspected shell-craters, explosions that fling both man and machine off the road are everyday occurrences in this job. Even if the man escapes unhurt, he can't foot the distance always, if the matter is urgent and there are miles to go. A special provision allows him the privilege of commandeering on such occasions any vehicle that may come in his way, whether it be horse or car, and whoever be the occupant.

1. *Despatch Rider* by W. H. L. Watson also published by Leonaur.

But——

There was a man once who, after tramping a couple of miles, could find no conveyance except that occupied by a general. He had courage, however, so he turned the general out, but oh what a tirade he brought on his own head! Afterwards he received a decoration for his audacity—when the general who fortunately had a sense of humour, had had time to recover his dignity and his temper. But I should hate to have been in his shoes. There were scores of us, of course, who ordered officers out of their saddles and diverted Army Service Corps trucks out of their destined route, and the curses that accompanied us on our journeys were not always pleasant to hear. If our instructor had substituted the word Diplomacy for Discretion, he would have been somewhat nearer the mark.

Again there is always the danger when the armies are on the move and not engaged, as they were later, on stationary destruction, of coming full-tilt into a straggling enemy troop.

"If you fall into the hands of the enemy," said our mentor, "destroy your despatch at all costs. Otherwise they may divert it to their own staff officers."

And then what a coup for the hostile strategists!

The usual method in such a case was to eat it—or rather to swallow it whole. The authorities, careful as usual of our digestions, as a rule wrote it on slim tissue paper that would almost melt in the mouth. Occasionally we had sufficient time to burn it, but not often. Occasionally, too, after destroying it as a precaution, we escaped. To meet this emergency which was also foreseen, we had orders to memorise our message always before starting, so that, in case of necessity, we could deliver it by word of mouth.

This rule in its turn led to further complications. The enemy knew that we had our despatches learned by heart. If they caught us and failed to find papers on our persons, immediately such a cross-questioning began as might well confuse even a seasoned criminal. Usually this was met by a closed mouth which no threat of death would serve to open. This, in turn, was met with a new ruse.

Before very thorough detective work had eliminated the menace, it was no unusual thing to meet men wearing our uniform and speaking our language but serving on the staff of His Imperial Majesty of Germany and not on that of King George. They would have been very glad to induce us to part amicably with our information. It was to circumvent such gentlemen that our last order was issued.

"The despatch must be delivered *in person* to the officer to whom it is addressed."

That was all. A unique simplicity marked our entire training. I decided, when they dismissed me in London, that it would take a fool to fail, and comparing my job with that of a private on the line, I felt that the War Office has no high respect for my intelligence.

Consequently as I looked round me that morning in the Havre Café at the men selected for the Cycle Corps, I was astonished at the lavish hand that would waste such material on such crude and casual work.

Out of the twenty assembled round me, not more than two had failed to graduate from either Oxford or Cambridge, and they were professional men of high standing in their own line, far above the type that might be deemed suitable for a competent "regular." Yet it was not so much trained intelligence that marked them as a group as a native ability, a certain keenness, a quality of initiative that would augur well for their readiness to meet an emergency. Physically, too, they were far above the average. About three of them fell short of a full six feet, a few would top that height by a few inches. All of them had proved their power to handle a gun with ease and shown an intimate knowledge of the moods and mechanism of motor-cycles. Which facts in themselves constituted a guarantee that they had lived rather largely in the open. If further evidence was needed, it was supplied by their appetites.

"*Voulez-vous donner moi un autre omelette?*" someone asks *Madame* in his best nigger French. He had already consumed two of

21

those substantial concoctions.

"*Mais, Monsieur!*" *Madame*, a plump, pleasing person, throws up her hands in horror, then remembering the instincts of her trade, runs off and is back with it in a few moments.

We are kept waiting by him—I learn later that his name is Poole—but not even our outspoken impatience could induce him to hurry. By the time he is finished, however, we have mapped out our routes, and by nine o'clock we are well on our way to Rouen.

It is a glorious morning. As we skim along the Rue de National, at full throttle, our spirits rise to the point of exuberance. Poole comes in for most of our surplus mental energy. Though he weighs about 250 pounds, he is riding a two and a quarter H. P. Douglas. Lawrence, a rather decent chap, offers to change, suggesting that the giant will never make the journey safe on his small machine. Indignant, Poole offers to race him to Rouen for ten shillings. Probably it was our desire to keep even with the contestants that brought us to that town in record time.

We arrive there about noon. It is another hour before we can find the T. O. Finally we locate him at a rest camp. It seems we are to be split up into sections along the various parts of the line. Poole, Lawrence, Grant and I are to be attached to the Second Cavalry Brigade. What luck! We have chummed up already. The next lap of our journey is to end at Amiens, where we will be directed straight to the fighting line. With luck we will be in the thick of it in another day.

4

It is August 25th, 1914. The "contemptible" British Expeditionary Force in France under Field Marshal Sir John French[2], is falling back before the numerically overwhelming German Army. From the Bavay-Maubeuge positions, the Second Corps under Sir Horace Smith-Dorrien[3] is retreating with orderly haste on the Le Cateau-Lanrecies line, their rear protected by a troop of cavalry.

---

2. *1914* by Sir John French also published by Leonaur.
3. *Smith-Dorrien* by Horace Smith-Dorrien also published by Leonaur.

And in a little farmhouse outside the former town, we are endeavouring to keep open communications in a temporary Signal Office, which leaves much to be desired. It is a dark, dirty hovel—one wonders at the family's reluctance to leave it—but our haste gives us no leisure to make a choice. In a remote corner of the kitchen the telephone operator has set up his switch on a wooden pedestal labelled "Jam." All along the wall, where still hang the cooking utensils, are ranged the telegraphers busily clicking their Morse keys. If visible evidence is needed of the urgency of their tasks, it may be gathered from the positions of their "Woodbines."

Instead of depending at the usual angle from their lower lips, they now stick jauntily behind their ears. Removed from the rest at a position near the window, the subaltern, a mere boy on whom responsibility has thrust age, sits anxiously poring over his maps and charts which tell of the positions of the lines and cables that an enemy shell may at any moment cut. Exhausted men on whose faces is a four days' growth of beard already matted with summer sweat and summer dust, heavy-eyed with sleeplessness, hollow-eyed with strain, they work with the dogged intensity of desperation.

"Line down on the road to Cambrai!" The man has to scream to drown the gun-roar.

With a curse a lineman sets out on his job.

"Last two D. R.'s not yet returned, sir." This message is meant as a reminder.

The subaltern looks up, pauses a moment as if to consider. Those despatch riders had left around five o'clock. It is now five-thirty, and Landrecies but five miles away! They should be back, unless some disaster has overtaken them. With sudden decision, the subaltern puts his head through the neighbouring window, and shouts in the general direction of the barn.

"Next two D. R.'s!"

At the sound of his voice four men spring to their feet. They had been lying full-length in the dirty yard, a somewhat cooler spot on this hot August evening than their quarters, the cow-house.

They are the remaining four of the six despatch riders who go to form this Motor Cycle Section. Let us present them before they are separated by the impending journey.

A couple of weeks ago a casual glance might have sized them up as gentlemen. Now even a close scrutiny might have measured them as tramps. True, they are clad in the uniform of the British army, but it is so covered with dirt as to have lost even its nondescript hue. The coat which a regimental tailor buttons smartly to the throat is thrown open to admit the sultry air; and a cap which a kind quartermaster places so trimly on the head, has been replaced by a large handkerchief, the colour of which is somewhat shady. Only the belts at the waist, from which depend business-like revolvers, and the maps slung securely over the shoulders, betray their fitness for the part they are to play, of which their bikes, much cleaner-looking objects than their owners, give further convincing evidence.

Who are they?

Well, there is Grant of the grey Scotch eyes, he from whose mouth hangs the dun pipe. And there is Hudson, the Belfast architect, now rivalling the grimiest of his bricklayers. And there is Harrison, the Cantab undergraduate, whose "people were so decent about his age." A scrupulous father might have held him back a couple of years. Lastly there is myself, a different person from that particular young man whom a short time ago we found looking so eagerly for a wash. Two weeks on the line have taught us the unimportance of such trifles as cleanliness. What's a dirty neck more or less, with death staring you in the face? Life itself is the possession that we have now learned to prize, and war, the great romantic adventure, has developed into a wild scurry to dodge the bursting of a shell.

Hudson and Harrison are the next on the list, but Grant and I accompany them to the farmhouse door, in case the subaltern might care to choose us for this crisis. Harrison has only arrived the day before. But it's his turn, and it seems he has to take it.

"You know what to do? That's right. Swallow it, if they get

you. Remember there are stray *uhlans* about, and Poole and Lawrence may have been caught. Now for directions. Go together to the cross-roads—those with the crucifix. Then take separate routes to the town. One of you may get through, if the two don't."

A pleasant prospect. The subaltern looks at Harrison, as he presents it, as if expecting some protest from the new recruit. But none comes, and the youngster, their age and station but for an accident, is suddenly moved to put out a hand.

"Good luck!" He gives each a grip in turn, before they double out of the room.

"Better strap the thing on your forefinger, old chap," advises Hudson with the wisdom gleaned in a week. He is referring to the precious tissue paper. "Handier to your mouth that way."

It takes them but two minutes to memorise the message and then they mount and are off on the darkening, dangerous road. Soon the crest of a hill hides them, and left alone, we lie down again. Among our new accomplishments is a facility for sleeping anywhere. But before slumber could come to soothe us, we hear voices nearby, and we listen. Some straggling Tommies are talking, and we are the subject under discussion.

"Not so bad for bloomin' civvies," says one, apropos of our departed friends.

We feel that we have accomplished much in these two weeks.

5

Ten-thirty—the guns are booming with ever nearer menace, utterly preventing our attempt at sleep. We are hourly expecting the order to move. Hudson, who is back after what seemed undue delay, reports a tough fight going on in Landrecies. We are holding a narrow street with a few machine guns on which the Germans continue to advance with their usual unlimited supply of gun-meat. It will be dead meat, piled high before morning, if we can only manage to hold out.

But where's Harrison? No sign of him yet either in Landrecies or on the road home. And Poole? Poole had delivered his despatch. So much Hudson had learned on his arrival, but of Lawrence no sign had been seen. We are discussing the probabilities of capture or collapse with a callousness that would have seemed brutal two weeks ago but which we have acquired with apparent ease of late, when there suddenly looms up out of the darkness of the road a motor-bike, carrying a strange object behind.

Soon a voice proclaims the rider as Poole, but what is the uncouth burden he is bearing? Flesh or fish; dead or alive? It answers both questions by jumping to the earth, when the bike comes to a jarring halt. It is the subaltern who has come out to take the air for a moment, who announces its identity by an ironical question.

"Been shrimping, Lawrence?" he asks politely.

Only then do we recognise our chum. A shapeless mass of slimy mud which clings to his clothes, his hands, his hair, his face, he looks for all the world like some prehistoric animal that has just risen from its oozy lair.

"Rotten duck-pond," he spits and shakes himself, as he tries to talk. "Been floundering about in it for hours. Dived into it headfirst, trying to take a nasty corner at full speed. The damn bike drove me down deeper—it came right on top of me. Must be a couple of miles of the stuff down under the water."

He was the first of us to get really intimate with the squelchy qualities of Northern French soil.

"Even when I got my head above water, I couldn't get my feet. The more I tried, the more entangled they seemed to become. Might as well have tried to walk with leaden shoes on."

How long it would have taken him to extricate himself alone is a question I leave to the imagination. It was Poole who finally rescued him after he had been struggling for what seemed hours. Even then it took strategy on the part of the two, as, indeed, it had taken foresight on Poole's part. He had delayed for some time in Landrecies, waiting for Lawrence to turn up. They had taken different routes on setting out. On the off-chance that an accident had happened, Poole had changed his road on the way home. Hence the rescue. And now, as Lawrence retires to the farm pump, we notice that his saviour looks rather white-faced and nervous.

"Anything wrong?" asks Grant.

"Oh, nothing much. Had a narrow squeak with some *uhlans*." He seems entirely indisposed to go into detail at the moment, so we open him a tin of bully and fetch him some water to help him in recovering his aplomb. If we thought thus to elicit the story, we were mistaken, for, even under the inspiration of a full stomach and a lit pipe, he refuses to satisfy our curiosity. We might never have heard what really happened, if a strange chance had not given us an inkling of the story, and forced him to confess to being a hero.

It was about half an hour later that a troop of our cavalry could be seen galloping over the hill. As they approached, we could see they were escorting some *uhlans* whom they hemmed in from all sides. Passing the Signal Office, the sergeant caught sight of our subaltern and immediately gave the order to halt. Then, riding over, he saluted, and explained that he had found the Huns prowling along the road leading from the Southeast to Landrecies. Now he would hand them over to the officer's charge.

They dismounted, preparatory to being led off to an inner room for the customary formality of being questioned. As they did so, one of them caught sight of Poole, and, nudging the other, he was heard to say in quite audible tones:

"There he is!"

But Poole, very busy for the moment with his carburettor, either did not hear or made a fine pretence of not doing so. Five minutes later, however, the sergeant's head appeared in the door-way, calling for the reticent hero. He departed, to return with a half-happy, half-sheepish grin.

"What's the matter?"

"Nothing. Some rot these Huns are talking."

But our curiosity was not to be stilled with such an excuse.

By dint of probing both him and the more eloquent sergeant, we got the whole story by degrees. Here it is. It is one of our reasons for being proud of Poole.

He had reached a cross-roads on his way from Landrecies. Shoot to the right—that was the turn for home. His bike took the curve at a dangerous angle, and, as he once more swept into the level, he raised his head to scan the new road. Lawrence was the object he was looking for, but what he saw at a distance of not more than a hundred yards was six *uhlans* seated on their fine mounts.

There was no time to turn—the speed of his bike decided that. And there was little time to think, not more, indeed, than a few seconds. Would he surrender! That might ensure his life, but the idea of a German prison did not entice him. In quick succession these thoughts shot through his mind, each second making a decision more difficult, as it brought him nearer his enemy. He was making about sixty miles an hour.

"I'll chance rushing them," he decided finally, and, banging open the throttle of his machine, he sent his speed up another five miles.

Forty yards from them, he could see them fingering their carbines. Thirty-five yards—he could see one of them, probably a sergeant, shouting an order to the others. Thirty yards—they were stretching in a line across the road.

Letting go one hand, he drew his revolver.

Twenty-five yards—he could see the two centre *uhlans* taking steady aim at his head. With a sudden jerk he drew himself erect in his saddle and then suddenly let his body fall along the top of his tank, at the same time letting go his revolver. He heard their bullets whizz by him—he had spoiled their aim—and he saw one man topple over, hit square on the chest, and the horse of the second rear and come down with a crash into the two *uhlans* on the left of the road.

Five yards from them—he could see they were in hopeless confusion, and, as he shot through the broken line exultantly—Poole avers it was the greatest thrill of his life—he sent two more bullets point blank at the men on the right, and tore past, a dark streak on the dusty highway.

Crouched over his handle-bars, muscles taut, nerves quivering, he strained his ears for any sounds that might indicate pursuit. They came. He could hear the pounding of horses' hoofs on the hard road.

"Galloping like mad," he commented to himself. But it would take some Centaur to catch up with his bike.

"*Whizz*"—another bullet shot past his ear. He crouched still lower on his saddle. And then—the gods were kind—there came another cross-roads. How he thanked heaven for these winding French highways and the hedges that would hide him on either side! Out of sight he was safe—a horse can't rival a motor-bike. So he came home with a whole but quivering skin.

"Of course it was the horses that did the trick," he explains amiably. "The bike and the shooting upset their nerves, so they pranced round a bit, and spoiled the blighters' aim. I'll buy a horse, when I go home, and pet him to death."

6

Off again. The inexhaustible Hun is determined to keep us moving. Our orders are to fall back in the general direction of St. Quentin-La Fère. Cable wagons dash out to reel in as much as possible of the wire they had laid just a day or two before. The operators are busy picking up their field buzzers and telephones. A merciful and ingenious government has reduced the weight of their pack to about three pounds. Soon they are all piled into the wagons, and we get off, a rather miserable train. Somewhere ahead of us is the brigade commander with his staff; somewhere in the rear of us is the retreating infantry.

All night and the next day we keep on the move, whither we don't know, but it is somewhere southwest. It is scorchingly hot, and the roads are thick with dust which stifles our nostrils and thickens our tongues. We pass through villages where our coming is the sign for increased panic. Stupefied women surrounded with wailing children are piling their household goods on to

29

trucks and carts. They block our way, but their misery hardly moves us at all.

At times we come to a crowd whose patriotism is greater than their panic. They greet us with the *Marseillaise*, an urchin or two already knows *Tipperary*. They offer us drinks, tobacco and food. All they ask is news. We have none save that our army is retreating. We give it, and the women set up a great "*La-La-ing*."

"Damn their infernal racket!" Grant growls at times. We are too tired to string our nerves up to the pitch of proper sympathy.

Soon I find myself journeying alone.

About four in the afternoon we had halted for rest, but I was no sooner off my bike than the signal officer came and handed me a message for the Guards Brigade. He had no idea where they were.

"Somewhere in France!" he declared jocosely. "I imagine they're off to the right."

As the Germans hadn't caught up with us, there was no danger of my capture, so he didn't think it necessary to send two of us. I took the road he indicated and wandered about for what seemed hours. Finally an Army Service Corps truck loomed up in the distance.

"The Guards? Someone said they were entrenching round Etreux." He pronounced it "Extroox,"' but we found it on the map. It was off in another direction. Luckily, however, it was on the Rue de National, so I found it without much delay.

My message was to a brigade major. I was unconscious of my general aspect, until I met his eye. I knew I was dirty, unwashed, unshaven. I'd had no sleep in three days, so my lids felt as if weighted with lead. My mind had ceased to work, so numb was my brain with fatigue. Only now for the first time was I conscious of my condition. But, as he handed me my receipts, he put a hand on my shoulder.

"I'm proud of you fellows," he declared in his hearty tone. "Our soldiers are magnificent, but then this is their business. You have no traditions to keep up." I flushed with pride under my dust, and he patted me on the back. When one is fatigued, one is foolishly susceptible to flattery.

"Pretty fagged, eh?" He inquired next. "Here, take a sip of this." He took out a glass flask from his pocket.

I'm afraid "sip" would not describe my drink. As I handed the flask back, a humorous smile twisted the corners of his mouth.

"Irish, eh?" He glanced at the flask. "Nothing like a drop of the 'crater' to put the heart in a man these rasty times." He gave me a slap on the back, before I mounted my bike, and I went off whistling on my way. I was glad I had been chosen for that trip.

I got back to my starting-place, only to find they had moved again. It was an hour later before I caught up with the rear of the Brigade, camping in the neighbourhood of Venerolles, where a halt had been called for the night.

We got a cow-house for a bedroom, but straw covered the dirt, and we were content with the mere fact that we had some hours to sleep. That night stands out in my memory, an oasis in the parched desert. The oasis fell from heaven.

Rain! It came in torrents! To welcome it, we walked out, throwing open our collars and the fronts of our shirts to let it fall on our withered skin. What a tonic it was! We were invigorated, men again. Our gratitude, however, faded next morning, when we had to set out on our road.

Perhaps you have ridden a motor-cycle over slippery surfaces, and you know what the slime does to the wheels. But try to imagine yourself keeping the bike erect on the slithery tops of cobble stones, not those smooth flat stones you find in England or America, but those round, uneven, beautifully curved cobbles standing anywhere from four to six inches out of the earth with which they pave the village streets in France. By noon my wrists had swollen to an unbelievable size from the effort of my task. I knew now why the foreseeing authorities had chosen strong men for the Despatch Corps. We were all but exhausted when we reached St. Quentin.

Our stay in the quaint old town, however, was destined to be short. The Germans were coming on pretty fast. Behind us we could hear the guns thundering out their terrific threat. There was nothing to do but keep moving. The sun had come out again, so we jogged along in our dull, damp misery, halting now by the roadside to eat such food as we had, or pulling up at a stream to bathe our heads in the cool water. A trip to a neighbouring town broke the monotony for us riders. Cable communications were out of the question for the present, with the Huns close on our heels. It was up to the Despatch Corps now to keep the small body of the British army articulate.

Le Fère! It is Saturday. At least so they tell us. We have time for a shave and a wash, with a fairly decent hot meal as meals go. We sleep in houses tonight, and come out in a square in the morning to catch a glimpse of a "*Taube*" overhead. It is no more than twenty-five hundred feet up. Instantly the Tommies straggling round start a perfect fusillade with their rifles, and succeed in doing more damage to themselves than to the Boche. Not to be outdone I whip out my revolver, and take a pot-shot in woolly West fashion.

"Ah, don't 'urt 'im, sonny," says a sarcastic voice at my side.

In my excitement I had forgotten the limited powers of my Webly.

By noon we are off again. A downpour catches us on the road, but we plod on, rather sick and disgruntled. So it goes for the whole week. Always the same order—to keep moving. Always the same accompaniment to our journey—the grim din in the distance. Always the same question in our minds—are we ever to be allowed to face them!

Courcy-le-Château, some dozen villages, Villiers-Cotteret—we tramp through them all. I touch Soissons and a few more on my side-trips. In them I pick up such food as I get at an *estaminet*. Sleep! rest! They are precious things these times. We get them by snatches at longer and longer intervals. And so we approach Paris—and the Marne. But that name means nothing to us yet.

At last—it is September, but we hardly know the date, so confused is our sense of time and so unimportant has it become—we receive the order to halt. Somewhere on our right we learn is the town of Courtacon, held by the Fifth Corps of the French army. Somewhere on our left is the British army and the town of Coulommiers. We, the Second Cavalry Brigade, wedged between the two, are the link that binds the great chain.

This time our Signal Station is set up in an open field. In one corner by a green hedge squat the telegraph clerks and the telephone operators, setting up their instruments as best they may. At some distance on the grass is our group of despatch riders, taking a snooze whenever we get a chance. It comes rarely. There is great demand for our services these days.

Two messages an hour—that is our average. In two days I cover some six hundred miles in my flying trips from one part of the line to another. Two messages an hour, day and night—there is to be no let-up for the present. We have forgotten that the dark should bring sleep, that the morning should bring breakfast and the noon lunch. Food we have come to regard as a gift straight from the gods. It drops on us like the manna from heaven, descending on us through the agency of an Army Service Corps truck. We eat it, when we get it, if we have the time.

France was being saved in those days, but how were we to know that? My first day was made memorable by a trip to the French lines—I had never before met our Allied fighters. The officer I wanted was absent, so a French despatch rider was deputed to take me to the man I sought. "The despatch must be delivered in person."

A slim, little, lithe figure on an equally slim bike which he rode German-fashion with arms aloft on high handle-bars and feet sticking up in the air, he skimmed along in front of me, a dainty butterfly leading a cart horse. Uphill I lost sight of him. Downhill I swept by him.

I was instructed to keep close behind him, but it was altogether too hard a job. We passed through a village, the name of which I never learned, and my eye was held by the sight of a squat, resplendent officer shining with a profusion of gold lace. I asked his name.

"Joffre!"

The man who was then saving France, and he was strolling at leisure through the street!

My second day was made memorable by an incident that held my interest. They were making history round me, but what was that to me? My attention was still occupied with comparative trifles. And yet, perhaps, this man whose story I am going to tell, contributed more than he or I knew to the victory on the Marne. At least it was such as he who made it possible.

I had delivered a despatch to another British brigade, when I happened to run into Hodder. He was sitting in the Signal Station, wounded. It was a bystander who told me the tale.

He had been riding hell-for-leather near a wood, when a German sniper caught him on the foot. A fine shot, when the target was a despatch-rider. Over keeled Hodder and his bike, coming to earth with a terrible thud. It stunned him for a moment. When he recovered his senses, he knew there was no chance for him to mount that bike again. But he couldn't walk, with his foot in that condition. Still there was the despatch. It must get through at all costs.

Down he went on all fours. There were three miles to his goal. He crawled into the wood which was plentifully scattered with *uhlans*. Luckily they were not looking to find a rider among the underbrush. It took him hours to get through, but he did it, His clothes were in ribbons; his face all scarred, and his foot—but that is better left to the imagination. He delivered his despatch. He got the D. C. M. But that was some time afterwards, when the great scrap was all over.

At the end of the second day we received the order to advance. Lord! How that order stirred our hearts! Move forward! It was the first time since we landed in France. We looked eagerly at one another, half afraid to surmise the truth. Had we really driven the blighters back? Had we actually stemmed the flood that was inundating France with fire and slaughter? Bit by bit the news filtered to us in confidential whispers. The tide had been turned on the Marne! But it was fully three days before we, partakers in the victory, knew what our efforts had helped to do. Paris had been saved. Now for the rest of France. Our task had only just begun.

CHAPTER 2

# The Author Assists at a Victory and Abandons His Bike for Better Things

1

We have beaten them on the Marne[1]; we have beaten them on the Aisne. We have fraternised with them at Christmas during a twenty-four hour truce and found them human in the matter of souvenirs. Their officers have assured us that we have not a chance in a thousand—quite politely, of course, but with absolute conviction. By March we're to be flying with the first Eastern winds.

Well, we've kept them sitting all winter in their trenches waist-deep in French and Flanders mud. Meantime, of course, we've been sitting in it ourselves, with occasional relief in the shape of a run to London.

The Motor Cycle Despatch Corps, having earned the particular praise of Field Marshal Sir John French, is unusually lucky in the matter of these reliefs. Besides fresh men have been coming out in droves, a fact which combined with the general quiet along the line, makes it comparatively easy for the old men to get leave of absence.

I get seven days' home. Lord! how they loved us in those days in London! Private cars meet us at the Charing Cross station. Pretty girls hurl flowers at our heads. Crowds of cheering, excited men and women block our autos and impede our egress

1. *1914: the Marne and the Aisne* by H. W. Carless-Davis also published by Leonaur.

from the station. But we don't mind. We sit in the tonneaus, grinning amiably, a little embarrassed, if the truth must be told, by this somewhat novel role of returned hero. Not that we dislike it, you know! Far from that! But we don't feel ourselves big enough for the shoes.

At the end of the seven days, so crowded that they fly by on wings, I go back and find strange changes on the line. It is now shortly after Christmas. The cavalry, of no use in this stationary warfare, has been dismounted, much to its chagrin. Now its members are squatting in the mud along with the hitherto despised infantry. Lord! what a fall was there!

Our section which, you remember, had been attached to the Second Cavalry Corps, has been split up and scattered along the line. I lose my friend Grant; we are assigned to different units, but at least he is within calling distance, whenever there is time to call. I am with a brigade attached to the Fourth Corps, and Grant with an adjoining one two miles away.

But things are not as they were. Excitement has given place to ennui. Each day is like another, endlessly boring with its uneventful routine. War has degenerated into a dull, drab affair, an unromantic contest, mainly with the elements, the element of mud putting up the best fight.

And so we come through the winter, a disgruntled, disagreeable crowd, lazy, too, and inclined to cavil at all orders. If they won't let us fight, then why the devil can't we go home? That is in general our attitude of mind.

Comes a rumour shortly at which we all sit up.

The Russians are doing great things these days—it is now well into the Spring. One of our trench oracles opines that we are going to help them. There is vague talk of a "push," a poke in the ribs, so to speak, which will remind old Fritz that we are still alive and keep his attention from wandering too exclusively to the East. The blighter must not get the habit of feeling at home in France or Flanders.

Immediately such a change is noticeable along the line as must have gladdened the heart of the high command. Our step is surer, our heads a little higher, and we work with a new and eager will. After all sitting in mud is no incitement to deeds of daring. The mere thought of a move bucks us up.

## 2

For three days now we have been preparing for the event. Not that the powers-that-be have deigned to take us into their confidence. They are far too aloof for that. But they can't hide the evidences all round.

Morning, noon and night we are riding with our messages, all of them marked "Priority," which means that they admit of no delay. And all along the roads leading to and from Neuve Chapelle there is unceasing motion, endless processions that block our paths and impede our progress. Ammunition trains, convoys, Army Service Corps wagons—they are all moving up, carrying supplies for men and guns. In our efforts to pass them, we occasionally find our- selves lying in the ditch, as a result of over- estimating the width of the French roads.

And Lord! what weather we are having! The heavens, disap-proving of our preparations, do their best to hinder them and harm us. They simply open, and let the water pour down on our heads. We slip and slither all over the roads, and our wrists ache with the effort of keeping our machines erect. But somehow we manage in spite of it all.

Never in the early dark days before the Marne have we been as busy as we are now. All through the night of March 9th and the following morning, I carry despatch after despatch—to an artillery commander, an A. S. C. officer, a battalion commander, over and over again. When finally day dawns and hell breaks loose, it is to find me with twenty hours' sleep in arrears.

About seven o'clock, or a little earlier, the thunder is loosed. The guns which for days have kept up a constant crackle, now burst into a deafening roar. As I scurry along the roads, shells whir over my head. Thank heaven I am not at the busy end of their range!

Seven-thirty the curtain lifts, then is lowered farther back. A signal that the infantry has gone over!

I am detailed to take a message to the Twenty-first Brigade, one of the first to advance in the fight. There is electricity in the air toay, the electricity of excitement. It quivers along my spine; it stings my fagged brain. My mind is clear with the horrible clarity that is often the result of lack of sleep.

I spin along and am suddenly made aware of the fact that not all the shells are coming from our side. Not twenty yards in front of me, I see a great "Bertha" burst.

*Plop!* it goes square in the middle of the road. I have plenty of time to stop and plenty of room to swerve. My hands make a motion as if to turn the handle-bars, but my eyes are rivetted to that hole in the road. A grim fountain is playing there, spewing up sprays of mud, clay, smoke, stones and pieces of shell. They fascinate me.

"Turn your bike," says my brain.

But my eyes are glued to the spot. Like the lady driver who is so anxious for the safety of a lamp post, I can't leave that crater out of my sight. Presently I am conscious that we are meeting. Headfirst I go into it, but I land on top of my bike.

"Of all the blamed fools!" I say angrily to myself. "One would think you never saw a shell burst before."

I pick up my machine. It is unhurt. I climb out, furious with myself and quite unable to explain the phenomenon. Why should any sensible man ride straight into a hole? I mount again. It must have been half an hour later that I noticed a certain awkwardness in one of the fingers of my left hand. I had broken or sprained it in the crash.

I get back to my section and hear the glad news. We're advancing. The reinforcements are going up. Everything is working like a clock, but the Boches are by no means beaten.

Off again on a message. The "Berthas" are still busy. One falls in a field adjoining the road on which I ride. Another whirs over my head, with a scream like an eagle's. Along the way I come on evidences of their work. Here is a horse's trunk from which the head and legs have been severed; there a man's corpse almost cut in two. But I am not at all shaken by such sights.

What's the matter with me? I should be terrified by all the rules of this game. I remember legends of brave men who not only felt but confessed their fears. Where is the panic that the novelists promised me? Why should I be losing all the thrills?

Here am I skimming swiftly over a shell-ridden road, cheeks ruddy that should be ashen, hand steady that should be shaking, vision clear that should be clouded, brain functioning that should be fuddled. Is my calm an abnormal calm, a calm keyed to a higher pitch perhaps than that with which we conduct our daily affairs? Or is it a callous calm bred of familiarity with horrors too often seen? Is nature so adjustable that she can become contemptuous even of death itself?

"You may be killed by the next corner," I tell myself earnestly. But my knees refuse to quake.

And then I come to the next corner, and suddenly my equanimity is lost.

For there by the roadside I see a rider lying on his face, a broken bike by his side. There is something familiar about that recumbent form. I dismount, turn it over, and recognise my friend, Grant.

So the rotters have got him! Grant of the grey Scotch eyes, the best chum man ever had! Got him and disfigured him—half his face is bashed in. My calm deserts me on the spot. Now I know why a brother joins to avenge a brother, and a father to take toll for a son.

Why am I not in the trenches with a bayonet in my hand! I despise myself now for a mere messenger. Good old Grant! And I must leave him who would never leave me, lying dead by the roadside to be picked up—"another casualty"—like the thousand others whom I myself have passed so callously at times.

"The chances of war!" How many times I have said the words! Offered them with a shrug of the shoulder as consolation on the death of a friend. A new pity, a deeper sympathy sweeps over me, as I mount reluctantly. They had never taken a friend of mine before. Oddly enough it never occurred to me that they might soon take me.

3

It is afternoon now. The dim sun is going down. I am sent on a double message that takes me through the town. First I am to report to the Lahore Division whose Signal Office, I am told, is in a cellar; next to the Twenty-fifth Brigade.

Poor Neuve Chapelle! Already its homes are in ruins. Hardly a stone is standing on a stone. Instead they are lying all over the streets. I have to zigzag to get through.

After much meandering and many inquiries—I meet only Indians on my way, and their English is as fluent as my Hindustanee—I spot the blue and white flag that marks the signal service. I deliver my despatch and start off again. I have been told that the Brigade is trying to force the passage of a bridge somewhere to the northwest of the Bois de Biez. I find them facing a fury of machine gun fire, and depart glad to be alive.

But my mind is still busy with its memories of Grant. I forget myself, my machine, my surroundings. I ride along mechanically—I must unconsciously have been riding slowly, when I am suddenly hailed by a shout. I look round and see the grizzled head of an old soldier stuck out of a half-ruined house.

"Move a bit faster," he cries, "faster, mate, unless you want to click."

Hardly are the words out of his mouth, when he drops with a moan. I turn my head almost involuntarily to see whence the shot came. *Ping!* a few sparks fly out of my handle-bars. On the spot my investigation ceases, and my chance friend is forgotten in concern of myself. Jambing my throttle wide open, I sprint for home, sending my speed up to some sixty miles an hour. But I'm not quick enough.

With a jerk my foot is lifted from the foot rest, as if by an invisible hand. My map case which had been lying flat on my back, switches round and strikes me in the face. Next there comes a sharp rap on my knee, as if someone had hit me with a stick. I wobble frightfully, but don't lose my equilibrium. Neither do

I relax my speed. At a record rate I regain the Signal Office, dismount, and flop on the ground. My leg seems as if suddenly paralysed. And I notice a patch of blood adorning my pants.

So a sniper has got me at last!

There is no pain, strangely enough, only a burning sensation. Again my natural curiosity asserts itself. I look at my foot, and find that my boot is minus its heel. So that accounts for the sudden jerk off the footrest. But why should they have caught me on the left side, when the shot came from the right? This puzzles me extremely, but there is only one explanation.

The bullet could not possibly have passed through the little space that the make of my machine leaves round the engine. Consequently it must have hit the ground underneath and ricocheted up to my foot. But even at that it must have made some extraordinary curves. Another aimed at my back must have hit my map case and flipped it round in my face. But what about my knee? Were they then firing from both sides? Impossible! I would have noticed that. But there is no one with whom to discuss the phenomena.

Someone is already busily bundling me into an ambulance which takes me to the Casualty Clearing Station. Being a light case, I am sent next day to a base hospital.

The Casualty Clearing Station, for all the horrible suggestion of its name, proved to be a place of exceeding beauty—a French *château* evidently belonging to people of wealth. As they lifted me out of the ambulance, I had a glimpse of smooth lawns and trees of magnificent stateliness.

It took but a few minutes to get me on an operating table. Only war could have brought it to such uses. In times of peace clicking balls would have had my place. I could see the billiard cues still standing along the wall.

Then as they ripped off my trousers, and loosed the bandages, I had my first sensation of pain. Began a search then for an elusive bullet which proved to be conspicuous by its absence. To help me through the ordeal, I was given a glass of milk and soda. Only its colour told me its identity. I seemed to have lost my sense of taste.

"Oh, you'll be all right in a few days, sonny," the surgeon assured me—he was a splendid looking man with a mane of white hair. "Just a flesh wound; they missed your knee cap by about two mms."

He thought he was consoling me, but alas! poor man! he was sounding the knell of my hopes. My eyes had been turned towards home. So they took me to bed, a saddened patient who had seen heaven and tasted its joys in anticipation, only to have the cup dashed from his lips. Instead I got a meal, consisting of broth, toast and an orange. That failed to interest me, for I had suddenly realised that for thirty-six hours I had had no sleep. I needed no rocking that night!

Next morning I was awakened all too soon. The hour was barely 6:30. I opened my eyes to behold an orderly standing amiably near my bed, bearing a basin of water. How that good-natured fellow irritated me with his officiousness! He would insist on washing me; and I would wash myself. I won out, and immediately justified his zeal by upsetting the water all over the bed. But at any rate I had not been treated like a baby!

While waiting for the ambulance train to take me back of the line, I had my first good look at my fellow sufferers. Including myself there were eight slight cases, but the others! God! that any man should look like them! Disfigured is scarcely the word to apply to them. Grotesque gargoyles—that was how they seemed to me.

On the train I was placed in a compartment with a man who had been a member of the Black Watch. One of his legs had been shot off. His face had been skinned, Lord knows how! And he had lost his right cheek. And he suffered! Oh! how he suffered! The train bumped and rattled the whole of the way, as only French trains can. It bothered me who was scarcely hurt at all. Now it would wring a groan from that poor remnant of a man, now a curse, now a cry.

At three that afternoon he died *en route*. We stopped, while they took away his corpse. His going left me sick and nauseated, and lonely—oh! so lonely. I think I would have cried with homesickness, if a trained nurse had not chanced to come by. She stayed with me for the greater part of the journey. What would soldiers do without these women? But how did they stand the sights that I had seen today, stand them night, noon and morning, as a war nurse must? I'm afraid my courage would fail me as such a test of human endurance.

Toward evening we reached Le Trepore, a beautiful hospital situated on the French coast. Its base is a cliff, some two thousand feet over the sea. They told me it had been a summer hotel, and a German still owned it. Now resident in Switzerland, he was getting 400 *francs* a day for its use by the British government.

A perfect army of nurses, doctors and orderlies met us. They were ranged in the big, broad hall. Then with a neatness and efficiency nothing short of miraculous, they despatched us to our different sections. Surgical cases here; medical cases there. How could they distinguish us so quickly?

By ten o'clock we were in our wards, small rooms of four beds each. We were put to bed, given hot milk and soothed to sleep. Could it be only yesterday that I was listening to the roar of guns? Was it possible that France still held such retreats as this? Yet, I suppose, we were not more than sixty miles from the actual firing line.

More comfortable than I had ever hoped to be outside of my home, I fall asleep, too lazy even to look around. I wake up again to be confronted by a smiling, familiar face. I rub my eyes, blink, provoke a boyish laugh.

Who is it? None other than young Harrison.

There is a bandage round his head, concealing a scalp wound received a few days since in the fighting round La Bassée. But how had he got to La Bassée? We had given him up for dead or captive on the night when he failed to return to our farm signal office from his mission to Landrecies.

Oh, yes, he has a story to tell. Here it is, as he told it to me.

As you remember he and Hudson had separated at a cross-roads. As you remember, too, there were *uhlans* about. Not for him the luck of Poole who had shot his way through. A bullet in his back tyre decided that.

"The first I knew of it," he says, "was a skid of my rear wheel. The ground seemed to rise up and hit me in the face, and then glide away again from under me. When I recovered my senses, I saw two Boches standing over me. Thank the Lord! I had the wit to stick my finger in my mouth, and swallow the despatch whole."

Then ensued a colloquy between the two, not a word of which Harrison could understand.

"We really ought to know their beastly language," he declares.

Finally one turned to him, went systematically through his pockets and then motioned him to walk on ahead. For almost an hour he trudged along the dusty highway, the *uhlans* on their horses bringing up the rear. He was hot, heart-sick and aching from his fall. But what bothered him was the question of where these fellows were taking him. He scanned the road for landmarks that might indicate his position, but none met his eye. They seemed to be cutting across country, skirting villages but still within easy distance of the fighting. For the boom of the big guns seemed to be growing louder instead of less, and he could hear the rattle of exploding shrapnel.

"It must have been midnight," he says, "when we came up in the rear of an infantry battalion which from the look of things was setting out on the march."

As they approached, one of the escorts threw himself off his saddle and walked towards the officer in charge. There ensued another colloquy, equally indistinguishable to Harrison. Then——

"Come here," said the officer in perfect English.

He approached, and once more they went through his pockets. Then he was ordered to take off his clothes.

"I thought the brutes only meant to make their search more thorough, so, of course, I complied very promptly. While I was doing it, one of their soldiers, at a sign from the officer, ran up to a motor lorry, took off a bundle, and brought it over to me. And can you guess what was in it?"

I give it up.

"A German private's uniform!"

Harrison stops for a moment as if the memory were too much for him.

"Even when they ordered me to put it on," he says, "I could scarcely realise what it meant. Can you think of me fighting on their side? I suppose they were too far from their base or something to send me back, but fancy putting me in one of their beastly coats! And God! how those brutes treated me!"

Too frank, too courageous to pretend any friendship, he glared at the men round. I can imagine the look on his young haughty face. An Englander! How they were hating us just then! But there was nothing for him to do but obey orders. So, with a German pack on his back, and the *Kaiser's* cap on his head, he started on his weary march.

"For a while," goes on Harrison, "I was wild with anger, but they soon cured me of that. I swung around once, when someone laughed behind me, but a prick of a bayonet brought me to my senses. Then someone kicked me in the shins, and another spat at me. I turned on him, and a howl went up. But a sharp order from the rear stopped that, and then they began growling like a pack of surly dogs. Dogs," he spits the word out viciously. "That's the only fit name for them. Lord! if our officers treated us as theirs treat them, we'd mutiny. At least, I would."

A nurse comes in just at this point, and notices Harrison's flushed face. She threatens to separate us, if there is any more excitement. "Bad for his head," she whispers to me. I suppose she is right, but I am longing for the end of his story. I get it along in the afternoon.

"I don't know how many days we were marching," he says. "To me it seemed like years. Of course, I was alone all the time. They gave me food, but I had to eat by myself. They treated me as if I had the plague. Do you think," he asks me earnestly, "we'd be as rotten as that, if we had one of them in such a fix? And not a smoke all the time! I wonder they didn't starve me or stick a bayonet through me. Sometimes I felt like doing it myself. I'm surprised I didn't, when I look back on it, but I suppose we all like to be alive."

This is a very much older Harrison than the boy I met last. Then he was eighteen; now he's thirty.

"We were way back of the fighting most of the time," he goes on, "though we could always hear the din of the guns. Then one day it seemed to come very near. Next I heard the shrapnel again, and then the ping of bullets. So I knew we were nearing the real fighting. Finally, about three o'clock on an afternoon, I saw a village in the distance through the shade of thick trees. And I realised that there was a battle on in that town. God! it was good to know that you were somewhere near, even if I was on the wrong side of the line."

Then began his real ordeal. He had re-entered the fight in the midst of a street scrap, one of those contests in which the houses on opposite sides of a street form the lines for the op-posing troops.

"Almost before I realised what was happening, I found my-self in a house. It was dark. They had closed those long French shutters, but presently I was close up beside one. Through the cracks I could see the street, very narrow and clouded with smoke. I kept on peering through—they had forgotten me in the excitement. Suddenly a head bobbed up on the opposite side. A Tommy! I could have shrieked with delight! But the next instant a red-black spot appeared on his forehead, and then the head disappeared. They'd shot him, the brutes. How I loathed them!"

Harrison stops for a moment, and there comes a glare in his eye. I'm afraid he's getting excited. I feel I ought to stop him, but I dread the coming of the nurse. The glare dies down, and I am relieved. In its place comes a look of determination.

"I just made up my mind, then," he says, "that I would not stay with them. I guessed that they'd kill me, if I tried to get across, but I decided to risk it anyway."

The door of the house had been blown open by a shell. This gave him his chance. He moved toward it, and presently caught sight of a window on the opposite side from which glass and frame had been shot out. Sprint across and climb through—that was his programme.

"No one was watching me," he explains, "and I'm a pretty good runner. So I tucked my head under my arm, and dived into the street."

For a moment no one fired, each side probably dumbfounded by the sight of this man dashing through No Man's Land. Then——

"*Rip, rip,*" spoke up the bullets from both sides.

But the moment had been enough. He was almost across. He felt a tickling sensation in his shoulder, a stab in his right foot, but he managed to muster up his energy.

"I'm British, British," he shouted for the benefit of his own side. "Don't shoot." By now the others had recognised him. Too late, however. He had dived through the window, and was safe on his own ground.

"When I woke," he finishes, "I was in hospital, and here I am again."

## 5

For five weeks they keep me in the hospital, part of the time in bed, part hobbling round on crutches. I learn to be thankful that I am not crippled for life. While Harrison is with me, we have excellent sport. There is one person who plays poker, and another who is learning golf. Each day the latter comes home with a tall story of some extraordinary stroke that he has mastered. Finally one fine morning he invites us all out to watch him, and we stroll out to the nine-hole course.

After much hemming and hawing, primping and prancing, he swings. Something hurtles through the air. For a moment he watches it with the critical eyes of an expert, then turns to us triumphantly.

"Well, what do you say to that?"

We say nothing, but our glance travels significantly but silently to the earth. His follows. There at his feet lies the ball. Perplexed he looks at his stick. The head is missing. In deference to his cloth, I refrain from repeating his comment. But that afternoon he deserts the links for the tennis court.

Soon it is discovered that Harrison's wound is not healing properly, so they send him to his native English air. I am chumless and consequently rather cheerless. What an appallingly monotonous thing convalescence can be! This early-to-bed, early-to-rise existence may be healthy, but it fails entirely to appeal to me. I begin to long even for the roar of a "Jack Johnson." So when at last I get my orders to march once more, I leave with a light heart.

My wound, I find, has placed me in the "veteran" class, so my duties are to be easy for a time. I am sent to the Signal Depot at Abbeville, to act as instructor to recently arrived "rookies." All morning I lecture to them on such diverse matters as their duty, the difficulty of being hygienic under fire; how they may accomplish the first and overcome the latter. In the afternoon, with the aid of maps, we plot out a line of our own. We pick different points to represent different brigades, each about two or three miles apart. Then I distribute fake messages, and find out how long it will take the novices to deliver them and return to their base. Some prove to be splendid messenger boys; others get the opportunity of returning to England, with the option of transferring to another branch of the service or doing a clerical job at home. But these latter are few and far between.

However, this job does not last long. Soon I am in excellent condition, a fact of which the authorities make me aware by informing me that I am to report to a brigade stationed outside St. Eloi. I am in no hurry now to get to the line, so I dawdle luxuriously along the road, a beautiful, wooded road over which the sun is shining amiably. Why must men mar such scenes with smoke and fearful slaughter? You see I have lost all my enthusiasm for the noble art of war.

At St. Pol I stop off for a good night's rest and a visit to a local "movie" house. I see Charlie Chaplin in the *Children's Auto Race*, and laugh at it with all the abandon of a regular "fan." Next morning I am on the road by six o'clock, and by eight I have arrived at my new station.

The Hooge show has about begun, so I am plunged into the thick of it promptly. The first day I ride to Ypres,[2] the sight of which fails to revive in me any respect for the great god, Mars. But not until next morning do my troubles really begin. It is August 1st, on which date we lost a recently achieved position by an overpowering attack of gas. For the first time in my life, I am made familiar with a gas mask, not the ingenious contrivance which our troops wear now, but a home-made variety that is anything but comfortable. It consists of a piece of saturated cotton wool tied up in a strip of gauze which is strapped over the nose and mouth.

I record a mental resolution that, law or no law, no dog of mine will ever again be subjected to the indignity of a muzzle. But I have seen some men already writhing in an agony of suffocation, so I submit to my mask without demur. I am inclined to think, however, that it affected my sight as well as my sensation. Else how account for the accident that presently overtook me?

I have just rounded the bend of a road. Yawning in front of me is a shell-pit, large enough, the Lord knows, to be seen even by a blind man. Yet it escapes my notice, until forcibly thrust on it. *Plop!* I go into it, again on top of my machine which, this time, succumbs under my weight. I have probably put on a few pounds in that excellent hospital. Anyway the front wheel crumples up like so much cardboard.

I get to my destination on foot, and return by the same method, to be met by an irate officer who gives me a very sound rating for the negligence to which he attributes my mishap. Didn't I know that it was a new machine, and very precious?

He gives me another, and dismisses me with a message and a

---

2. *From Messines to Third Ypres* by Thomas Floyd also published by Leonaur.

warning. I start off in a downpour of rain, and am not more than half an hour on the road when I come plump into a five-ton truck. I try to pass it—on the wrong side of the road. To punish me, it crowds me into the ditch. In spite of the warning I prefer my own safety to that of the machine. I jump clear, and the back wheel of the truck passes over the gear box of the bike, which also crumples up like so much cardboard. I am debating the desirability of footing the rest of the journey or commandeering the truck on the spot, when I perceive another motor cycle approaching. The rider is good enough to give me a lift.

I deliver my message and once more return to my headquarters on foot. And oh, the dusting down I get now! My officer—recently arrived and in consequence most conscientious—threatens to report me for carelessness. How I should like to be that man's superior for a few minutes! I'd teach him to treat "veterans" with a little more deference! The worst of it is that I know he is quite right, and I am very conscious of the fact that for a seasoned cyclist I am doing very badly.

However circumstance forces him to entrust another bike to my bad hands. This time I am sent to a small village on the north of Ypres. I get through safely and am about to leave the Signal Office, when someone stops me. Would I take a message to a battery commander located in a dugout on the main road midway between this point and Hooge? I agree, of course, on the one condition that my brigade is notified as to my delay.

*En route* I become painfully conscious of the extraordinary activity of the Boche guns. The shells whir over my head at the rate of sixty to the second. I cover my mile or two at about the same speed. I get through, get my receipt and return in safety. The incident passes from my mind. Pass four or five days with the same dangerous routine. These are hot times for the town of Hooge. At the end of this time our Brigade is relieved, and we retire without reluctance for a rest.

It is a couple of mornings later that a large and hirsute sergeant major wakes me up with the message that I am to report at eight sharp to the brigade signal officer.

"What for?"

"Don't know, but you'd better not be late."

That sounds promising, and sets my brain to work. Had that blankety-blank rookie officer reported me after all? If he had, well, I only hoped that we would both survive the war and that the gods would be kind enough to make his path lie near mine! Nothing for it, however, but to report in time. I do so. The officer looks me over.

"Oh, you're Corcoran?"

"Yes, sir"—his tone relieves my tension.

"Well, at 8:30 you're to see the brigade major. See that you get there on time."

More mysteries! Again I report promptly, and once again am met with a smile.

"You've been recommended for a commission," he informs me amiably. I suppose I look puzzled, for he adds the explanation: "For good work—carrying despatches under fire."

The commission, he goes on, is to take effect from August 17th. It is now August 20th. He shakes my hand, and wishes me all sorts of good luck. I depart, extremely perplexed.

What else have I been doing since the beginning of this business but carrying despatches under fire! What else had I been doing, when I received my wound? I decide that strange are the ways of the War Office. While I am deciding it, my feet lead me involuntarily to the Signal Office, where the signal officer is still sitting. I put the problem up to him. He smiles.

"Do you remember," he asks, "on August 1st delivering a despatch to a battery commander outside Hooge?"

Of course I do, but what of it f

"Well," he explains, "you may not be aware of the fact but six men had tried to carry it before you, and every single one of them was killed."

"Good Lord!" the ejaculation comes out unconsciously. There can be no doubt of the fact that ignorance often brings bliss.

Thus unwittingly and involuntarily do I become a hero in spite of myself. Thanks be to Mars! He is henceforth my friend.

Next morning, August 21st, I receive my discharge, and am sent back to England for an officer's training. Automatically my commission is in the Signal Service of the Royal Engineers. My orders are to report on arrival at the Signal Depot at Fenny Stratford, where I find Lt. Col. Lister as O. C. at the time. He grants me five days' leave in which I may see my friends and get my new uniform.

I rush down to Devonshire where my people are just then, and live for the first three days in a blur of hand-shaking, hugging, kissing, questioning, from which I finally escape to London. Follows a hectic time with the tailor, a round of dining and dancing. I find no let-up in the old life here. But oh, how the good time flies!

Then on the fifth morning, togged out in my new trim dress, I report for duty at my station. I have quite decided, of course, by this time that I shall have at least four months at home. They can't turn out completed officers in a shorter period than that. So I begin to plan for myself all sorts of pleasant surprises. Let all those eager youngsters who are so anxious to get across, hurry over, if they want to. I'll take my time. I am quite aware of the fact that the Boche will be still waiting there, and far be it from me to unduly hasten the meeting!

At Fenny Stratford, an adjutant takes me in hand, and inculcates the first principles of such important trifles as *esprit de corps*. Then he turns me over to the officer in charge of the school. He puts me through my paces to see what I know. Ever done any telegraphy? Ever heard of such things as circuits? I inform him that I have taken an electrical course at Cambridge. Which elicits an exclamation of pleased surprise.

"Then, of course, you've been in touch with the signallers all the time in France. You know about cable laying, air line rigging, etc.?"

I allow that I am at least initiated into these intricate rites.

"Ever ridden a horse?" he asks me next.

"Well, I ranched in Bolivia for a few years."

"Good! It won't take you any time to get onto the mounted drill. I should think you'll be through in about ten days!"

Through? What did the man mean? I don't know what sensation my expression signified, but he goes on pleasantly, in his reassuring voice.

"Oh, yes, another three weeks ought to see you back on the line!"

My Lord! why haven't I learned to keep my mouth shut? Once more my Spanish castle comes tumbling about my ears. I always thought I was a fool; now I know it.

My stay at the depot is not prolonged over two days. Then I am hustled off to Haynes Park, Bedfordshire, and put into a drill class that has commenced the same day. I get a mount. Poor beast! If he were mine, I'd either shoot him or pension him for the rest of his natural life. However, having taken one look at my sergeant major riding master, I keep all such reflections to myself. What a martinet the man is! And heavens! what a voice and tongue!

"Now, gentlemen," he bawls, before beginning the class. "You're 'ere to learn to ride an 'orse, and I'm 'ere to learn ye to do it. I know very well as 'ow ye're officers, but the arf hour ye're with me, please remember ye're my pupils. Now then, all who think they can ride, ride out in front."

For a few seconds I hesitate. The man has cowed me. Then I take a chance with two others.

"Where did you learn to ride?" he asks me sarcastically.

"In Ireland and then in Bolivia."

"Oh!" he turns to the man next me, a chap named Finney.

"I'm from Northwest Canada," Finney informs him.

"I ain't inquiring about your birthplace. I'm asking if you can ride."

What a terrible man! But Finney is not terrified.

"Well, I've been at it twenty years," he replies with a drawl.

The sergeant major turns to the third. Poor chap! he had learned in a London riding school. We are put through our paces in front of the class. Finney and I manage to qualify, but the rider from London! He is informed quite audibly that when it comes to managing horses, he may be an excellent master of his mother's clothes horse.

As the first six of the ten days are devoted to teaching the others to sit astride, Finney and I are dismissed. We have some grand gallops all over the country. What a magnificent horseman that man was! I doubt if I have ever seen his equal. Then for the last four days we are told to chip in, and pick up the mounted drill required of a signal officer. It isn't much, and the horses, well trained brutes, carry out the orders on their own account. That over, we are handed our certificates—that is, all of us who manage to qualify. Follow seven days' leave, another oasis in the desert, from which we return to be placed on the list for the overseas draft.

For a week I do such routine duty as that of orderly officer or paying billets. This last is incidental only to certain depots and camps. Where the number of men is too great for the regular accommodation, they are placed with private people round, a regulation which adds from fifteen to twenty-two shillings weekly to the coffers of the families chosen for the honour. An officer is detailed to distribute the money.

At the end of the week, I am chosen with several others for the doubtful honour of a Cook's Tour. This tour consists of a two weeks' visit to the firing line, and its object is to give young officers an idea of their future duties, before they are entrusted with a section of their own. At the conclusion of the tour, they return to England,—sometimes. My case, of course, came among the exceptions. Some people have none of the luck!

CHAPTER 3

# In Which the Telephone Proves Its Utility and Instability

1

Our Cook's Tour, not being supervised by the experienced gentleman himself, fell apart very early in the game. In fact when I left Boulogne, I was a party of one, with a ticket for the First Army Headquarters stationed near Bethune. In that well-shelled town I found a host of determined tradesmen trying their best to carry on business as usual. A very lively business it was! Whenever the vivacious barber at the corner of the square laid his razor against my well-lathered cheek, I began to wonder whether a "*whizzbang*" would not finish the job for him. But his hand was none the less steady for that possibility, nor the flow of his language the less fluent. Too bad I could not catch a word of what he said! Not that he minded! No, indeed, he kept right on talking, thereby making me feel quite at home.

My stay in his town, however, was destined to be short. In a few days Mr. Cook decided to send me further. This time my ticket was for a point nearer the line, the rear of the now famous town of Loos. Just then we were preparing, as you say, to "put the place on the map." My part in the preparations was to be contributed under the title of Supernumerary Signal Officer to the Seventh Division.

It was early—too early—on a September morning, when I started on my journey from Bethune. The road I was to take launched out from the great square, a peculiarity it had in common with about a hundred others. Round and round I flew on the motor bike that furnished my means of transit, but no distinguishing mark of my street could I see.

Meantime the black sky had turned to grey, and the .grey to green, before my eye finally lighted on a sleepy and sullen sentry who had probably been admiring my gyrations for the past hour. In reply to my questions, he raised a lazy finger and jerked it over his shoulder. In no measured language, I tried to indicate what I thought of him and his square. Rotten, tricky place! I hoped the Boche would get it, but somehow they never get the things you could best spare.

Arrived at my destination, I found a batman and billet awaiting me. My quarters were to be in an old French farmhouse on the main road between Vermelles and Noyelles.

"Well, here I am, no longer a free-lance but a fixture in the fighting forces, with my own small but significant part to play in the gory game. But before I proceed to describe the action, let me picture to you the *mise en scène.*

## 2

Being a typical French farmhouse, it is also typically Irish. That is to say, judged by the conventions of most other countries, it puts the cart before the horse. The first object to assail your senses—it attacks two at a time—is the garbage pile which the family heaps up in public. This flanks one side of the rambling yard. Most of the remainder is given over to a species of mudbath, not to be recommended, however, for cases of rheumatism. In it the non-human live stock disport themselves daily. At the back of this yard, and fronting the gate, comes the house, with its various adjuncts. Lastly there is the family which emerges to view by slow degrees.

There is *Madame,* the stocky, stolid, and dark- eyed, around whom in the absence—and perhaps in the presence—of *Monsieur,* all activities pivot. There is another *Madame,* presumably her mother; and another, still older—but here we stop. The degrees of this *menage* could be distinguished only by a genealogist. But, as an outsider, I should say that at least four generations lived under that roof. One of the youngest is the first to meet my eye.

I was riding toward the house, when the strangest little rag-bag swung round a corner into my sight. It was his whistle that first attracted my attention. With head thrown back and chest thrown out, obviously in imitation of his friend the Tommy, he was shrilling not unmusically the then popular tune:

" Hold your hand out, naughty boy!"

As he came nearer, I was able to distinguish his wardrobe. On his head was a Tommy's cap, probably rescued from a rubbish pile. Round his body was a Tommy's groundsheet in which three holes had been made to allow egress for his head and arms. On his feet were some gumboots several sizes too large for him, kept in place by some dirty spiral puttees. And around his neck—it took some time to distinguish this ornament—was a circular loaf, one of those horseshoe affairs that you see so often on the tables of France. Jean—or was it Joseph?—was returning from market.

I think I recognised that loaf later when I sat down to table in the spotless kitchen and living room of the family. But did I or my fellow officers remark the fact to *Madame?* Not we! We would not dare, even if we so desired. But we did not desire. All three of us are old-timers in this show, and such details as a little dirt from Jean's—or is it Joseph's?—neck do not in the least disturb our excellent appetites.

There is Harry Wills, a lieutenant from the Norfolk Regiment, one of the earliest of the "old contemptibles." Shattered nerves had sent him home to England. Now he's here to finish his "rest-cure" amid the autumn amusements at Loos. Little joke on the part of the R. A. M. C.! In contrast to him comes Collins, a second lieutenant from South America. A shell burst near Collins two days ago, making a crater as big as a house.

"Damn nuisance !" said Collins, turning nonchalantly around. "There was a nice shady spot to smoke in, under those trees."

I share a room with Collins for a night. Then my batman, a wily beggar who can manage even *Madame*, secures an outhouse for my special accommodation. I call it an outhouse, but in reality it consisted of four walls and a roof. The floor is of cobble stones, but they are beautifully cool. On this my bed is erected, and I live *en prince*. In other words, I have privacy—a prized possession.

Last evening I was sitting here, trying to write home, when a perfect chorus of voices, male and female, floated on the evening breezes to my ear. They came from the direction of a field near-by. I peeped out, and beheld this pleasant scene, calculated to gladden the hearts of the believers in the *entente cordiale*.

On a ditch sat Angele, eldest daughter of the house, as yet scarcely sixteen. With her was a brother and round her three Tommies. In inharmonious unison they were "rendering" the popular air, known to us as "We won't be home till morning." Angele and Frere gave it in the words of their native land, "*Malbroeck s'en va t-en guerre*" and not a verse did they miss, nor a line. But the Tommies, I noticed, though trying to prove their right to the song, knew no more than the first line which they repeated *ad lib*.

"Angele! Angele!" shrilled a voice across the yard. It was *Madame*, interrupting the concert. Eldest daughters have little time for such indulgence. Immediately Angele hopped off her perch, and presently I heard one of those seemingly interminable and unintelligible monologues rendered by the mother of the house. Was she scolding or merely ordering? It might have been either. I confess *Madame* always baffled me completely. Like all foreigners, I had thought of French women as flighty. Yet she, a very typical sample, I am told, of her sex, was the stolidest human being I ever beheld. I was in her kitchen on one occasion when a shell burst in the yard, damaging the wall of the house and breaking every pane of glass. She was cooking her everlasting soup at the time. She looked at the kitchen window, staring silently for a few moments at the hole, and then calmly proceeded with her stirring.

Not a sound, not even a sigh, escaped her. But I should not like to be nearby when *Monsieur* returns to lift the burden from her shoulders, when the terrible tension at length relaxes, and releases nature from its strain. I should be inclined to predict that she will celebrate the occasion by a wild burst of hysterics. Meantime there is not a tear in her eye. More power to her, as they say in my country! Though I can't fathom, I can at least admire her.

But to come back to the business on hand. As I have said, we are in the throes of preparation for one of the greatest pushes in the war. My duty, as Supernumerary Signal Officer, is to superintend the laying of cable that will insure telephonic communication both behind and on the line.

3

Our playful friends, the infantrymen, have their own names for our corps. They call us the "Iddy-Umpties" or the "Buzzers." To the War Office we are known as the R. E. Signallers, and you may recognise us easily by the blue and white bands that adorn our strong left arms.

A much-abused person is the "buzzer." In the world military he occupies much the same position as that enjoyed in the civil community by our friend, the "Hello girl." Like her he is accustomed to all degrees of language, from the zero to the boiling or bubbling point. Unlike her he is untrained to the niceties of etiquette; he has not learned, so to speak, to turn the other cheek. "Please" and "thank you" do not rise naturally to his lips, when an impatient conversationalist consigns him to torrid regions. Indeed, at times he is apt to reciprocate the wish and he allows you small chance of turning to the "manager" for relief. Such a desire would probably provoke on his part a loss of hearing. Still, as I have said, he is much abused; also he is much used in the modern army.

His headquarters is a Signal Office, designated by a blue and white flag. His habitat may be anywhere according to the exigencies of the moment. The Signal Office, however, is always attached to a unit, usually to a brigade headquarters from which all activities radiate. Hence cable links up communications with the battalion headquarters and with company headquarters all along the actual trenches. Hence airline connects up the brigade with division headquarters, and division headquarters with corps, and corps with army and army with general headquarters and G. H. Q. with the War Office.

In short it is the "buzzer's" business to link up the whole line. He is an indispensable person, as you may see. But for him you would never read those daily bulletins telling you what the troops are doing on the front. A ubiquitous person, he is everywhere at once, letting the right hand of the army know what the left hand is doing, and letting the world know what both are accomplishing at the same time.

This story, however, not being concerned with the High Command, we will return forthwith to the brigade headquarters to which my particular section was attached. Here the personnel of the Signal Office consisted of telegraph clerks, telephone operators, lineman, messengers and despatch riders. A subaltern, assisted by a senior sergeant, acted as "boss." In conjunction with him but not subordinate to him, worked two cable sections, two airline sections and a wireless section, each controlled also by a subaltern.

Brigade headquarters, naturally, controls the whole brigade, which means as a rule that it commands about three miles of actual fighting front. All its business is transacted over the telephone, the operators taking their turn at the Signal Office and on the line just as the "Hello" girls do in New York City. In the trenches these operators are as a rule infantrymen, the most intelligent of the company being chosen for the job. (Loud cries of contradiction from the infantrymen!) The most intelligent, indeed, are none too good. Seated in dugouts which also fly the blue and white flag, they are under the control of the R. E. officers who see that the work is done properly and the lines always kept in repair.

When Fritz is taking his intermittent naps and sometimes even when he is about his *Kaiser's* business, the work of these trench operators consist in conveying such messages as the non-arrival that morning of the colonel's clean socks, the non-appearance of the company's plum and apple for tea, with an occasional detail concerning the havoc of a Boche shell. The speed of his work is, as a rule, about fifteen words to the minute. The regular R. E. signaller's is anywhere between twenty-five and thirty-five. He, of course, is a professional. The instrument on which the message is sent can be used either for telephone or telegraph. The operator decides which shall be used. It depends largely on his mood or his attitude of mind toward the sender.

When, however, our side has decided to get busy, a new batch of signallers is prepared for the event. Then as the waves of the infantry roll over No Man's Land, these men bring up the rear, reeling out cable as they go. Behind, the old operator remains at his old position. If a Boche trench is taken, then a new operator is there installed. He connects up with his old trench, which connects up with the Battalion Headquarters which connects up with the Brigade which is thus connected with the attackers. When a big "push" is on, the same principle is pursued, with the difference that the work is done on an infinitely larger scale.

Should the cable that is thus laid collapse for any reason—there are many usually why it should—then the safety of the whole section is threatened. If battalion headquarters and through battalion, brigade, is not acquainted with the movements of the troops; if they do not know the strength of the resistance, the approximate number of the casualties; the need for reinforcements, whether of men or guns, then the position of the Tommies is highly precarious. Suppose the attack has been successful and they are ready to advance further, then reserves must be brought up behind.

Suppose the line is breaking and there is danger of their being driven back, then assistance must be rushed to them without delay. But suppose the communications give way, and their needs cannot be made known! Well, the inference is too obvious to need mention. The signallers, as I have said, are the "nerves" of the modern army. Without them it is paralysed, and might as well be dead.

Later in this story we shall see what part the wireless plays in the supplying of the nervous system. For the present our business is with the cable section. It is to this that I was attached at Loos both before and after the scrap. My job was the superintending of the laying of the cables, seeing that they were put in the safest places, that they were mended when cut, that they were not earthed, thus making conversation undistinguishable. A nerve-racking job, a nasty job, rather tiresome and thankless, but entirely necessary, as are so many jobs in this romantic business of making war.

Now the Engineers, unfortunately, are not the only people who find it necessary to lay cable for the purpose of signalling in France. A little incident will explain the necessity for making this statement. Casual infantrymen are apt to confuse skilled with unskilled labour, and lay the sins of the latter at the door of the first. Needless to say, we are the party with the grievance.

I was invited to dinner one evening with the brigade mess. For twenty minutes we waited patiently in a sort of ante-room for the arrival of the brigadier, in whose absence we could not eat. He is a red-faced man at his coolest moments. When he arrived, his complexion rivalled that of a lobster or a beet boiled to a turn.

"G—d—it! I'd hang every one of them, if I had my way," he spluttered, as he strode down the room.

"What's the matter, Sir?" enquired some venturesome person.

"Matter? Matter?" he re-echoed the question. "What do you think, Sir? That b—— cable, of course. Outrage! That's what it is, leaving it lying about like that. Hit me first on the head. Then caught me on the foot and threw me headlong into a trench."

His attire, to say the least, was disordered. Someone glanced significantly at me, but I merely elevated my chin to express my supreme indifference. There was no opportunity at the moment to explain, but I take occasion to do so now.

That cable, my friend, belonged not to us but to the gunners. They use it to connect their batteries with the forward observation officer; also with the battalion commanders. Their method is to string it up on poles, each about eighty yards apart. Should a shell cut it, or should it become broken in another way, it will naturally sag to the earth. Do they mend it? Not they! They have no reputation to sustain in the matter. So their simple method is to let it sag, string up another. This in turn is broken. They let that sag, string up another, and so on *ad infinitum*, until finally their poles assume the complicated appearance of the mast of a sailing ship gone mad.

As an officer aptly expressed it one evening:

"The Boches may rush our first line; they may penetrate our second and pierce our third, but, as long as the gunner's cable is somewhere in the rear, England can always feel herself secure."

And now let me describe our more skilled and elaborate method.

From general headquarters up to brigade headquarters our telephones are connected by airline, a comparatively stationary and safe method of communication. From brigade headquarters to battalion headquarters—that is, from two or three miles behind the line right up to the trenches—cable has to be used for various reasons. The chief reason lies in the fact that it is the quickest and easiest method, easily laid, easily raised, according to the exigencies of the moment. These two points are, of course, movable. In fact, they may be changed within an hour.

A cable detachment consists of ten men, eight horses—four riders, four draft—and a wagon, the leader and the near wagon horse having drivers mounted. The wagon carries a number of poles for bridging crossings and four drums of cable, each containing five miles of insulated copper wire. The inside end of each drum is connected with the wagon and contact is made with a telephone on the boxseat.

Suppose the cable is to be laid between points A and B. The

loose end is paid out and man No. 8 (Nos. 9 and 10 being mounted on the draft horses) connects it with a telephone and remains at point A, while the wagon moves off at a trot.

Man No. 1, who is mounted, now rides on ahead, to pick out the most suitable road to travel. Man No. 2 works the telephone on the wagon, constantly keeping in touch with point A. Man No. 3 sits in the wagon, easing the cable off the drum. Nos. 4 and 5 sit in the wagon, armed with mathook and spade, ready at any moment they reach a crossing to jump down and dig a small trench. Nos. 6 and 7, both riders, bring up the rear, each carrying a crook stick. This consists probably of a broom-handle fitted at the end with an iron hook.

Should the route lie along a straight, unshaded road, then the duty of the rear riders consists in seeing that the cable does not fall directly in the line of traffic. Usually they push it into the ditch. Should a hedge, a small tree or some other standing object cross their path, then the crook comes into play. With a lift of his arm, No. 6 swings the cable aloft; should he miss, No. 7 takes on the job. If the road takes a curve, giving the cable a tendency to drag, then these two dismount and tie it at the side either to a branch or a stake stuck in the ground.

Suppose they come to a crossing of no great size, then out hop Nos. 4 and 5, dig a trench usually about four inches deep, and bury the cable to preclude any danger of its being cut by a passing vehicle or a horse hoof.

Having buried it, they then tie each end to some object near-by, so that the cable cannot be pulled out of its grave. This operation completed, the wagon moves on again.

Should the crossing, however, be large, or should a brook come in their path, then the cable is not buried but borne overhead. In this case it becomes the duty of Nos. 4 and 5, assisted by Nos. 6 and 7, to erect two poles, each about eighteen feet high, on either side of the crossing or water—an operation that takes about forty-five seconds. The rate at which cable can be laid by this method averages about six miles an hour.

In the trenches, naturally, this is out of the question. Horses and wagons have no room here, so a "man pack" takes their place. Four men go to make up this detachment. No. 1, whose duty it is to pay off the cable, carries his equipment strapped to his back. It is done up now in a reel, consisting of about 1,800 yards of 18-gauge, a smaller one than that used in the wagon set.

No. 2 here leads the way, fixing little wooden pegs in the sides of the trenches. No. 1 comes next, paying out the cable as he goes. Then come Nos. 3 and 4, who tie up the cable to the wooden pegs affixed by No. 2.

Shell-fire may at any moment, of course, cut through this cable, and various devices have been introduced to lessen the danger of the communications being destroyed thereby. For one thing, the cable is always laid in loops, one of which may be trusted to preserve the contact, though all the others be cut. This has been found effectual even in severe fighting.

But no method has yet been discovered to lessen the dangers nearer home. Even in the trenches it is necessary at times to appeal to the gods to save from our friends as well as our enemies. For often the sight of our cables remind a strolling infantryman that his shoe is sadly in need of a string. *Snip!* and our cable has supplied one.

Such accidents, combined with the unusual activity of Fritz, served to enliven the monotony of the days before Loos. There were others, however, more mysterious that also disturbed our peace, the disconcerting cause of which we discovered only after much damage was done.

A few hundred yards from our house there was a curve in the road, prettily bordered on one side by a clump of thick bushes. Beyond this curve stood a small hut, tenanted by an old shepherd who seemed to be wholly doddering and half dumb. His flock, sadly depleted by the advent of shells, he used to tend in a field adjoining the hut, the same field in which stood the clump of bushes.

Now this road led directly to the back of our line, so parties of Tommies and their officers were daily tramping over it on their way to and from the trenches. But not a party passed for days without losing an officer. Usually he was shot in the back.

For a time we stood it. Then an enterprising young subaltern decided to take the matter in hand. Receiving the necessary permission he and a friend took refuge in the shaded ditch that bordered the shepherd's field. For their trip they chose an hour when they knew a party of men would be passing along the road toward the line.

Crouched in their corner, they could hear the tramp of the Tommies' feet, an occasional whistle and the buzz of conversation. It came nearer and something stirred in the bushes. Up crept the two, keeping close to the wall.

Presently the men swung round the curve. As they did so, an arm became visible in the clump, holding a rifle in position. Then the subaltern threw discretion to the winds. With a bound he was in the bushes and the rifle was in his hands. The next instant he was grappling with the old shepherd. But the odds were on his side.

The old chap was a spy, and the handle of his harmless crook which it is the custom for shepherds in France to carry supplied the rifle that had been shooting our precious officers. But he had shot his last. The subaltern saw to that.

4

Well, it is September 24th, and our preparations are complete. All the cables have been laid; all the men been notified of the positions they are to occupy tomorrow. The particular sector whose communications are in our hands lies facing the famous quarries north of Hulluch. God grant we may be occupying them by next sundown! The infantryman is equally ready for his task. In my travels along the trenches, superintending my own men, I have caught glimpses of the efforts he is making. Here is a party filling piles of sandbags; there another serving out ammunition and bombs. A third is concealing the long iron gas cylinders. We have adopted the Hun tactics at last. It is a difficult but all-important matter to get these cylinders in a safe place. Should a shell hit them, we would be "hoist with our own petard." Finally it is decided to bury them under the firing-step, the most convenient and best-protected spot in the trench.

At 7:30 tomorrow morning the Loos ball will begin. The band has already begun to play. For the past month the artillery has been tuning up. Over the seven-mile front on which our advance is to be made, thirteen hundred guns have been pounding out their promise, sending intermittent samples of the music we may expect at the rate of three hundred rounds per gun. Now the intervals are growing shorter between items; the rounds have increased to five hundred. They are rending the very sky with their screams.

Meantime, of course, Fritz has not been backward. He is preparing a little pleasantry of his own.

*Whizz! bang!* The little hill behind our house has suddenly been transformed into a hollow. *Pip! Squeak!* A neighbour's hut is levelled, and in its place yawns a crater containing hut and inhabitants. Madame, the stolid, is already poorer by the loss of a barn, and our men are looking for other billets. Scully, my batman, robbed of his home, decides to share the one he has procured for me. Like the gentleman in the scriptures, he takes up his bed and walks. Now his straw is lying in a corner on my nice clean-cobbled floor. But he's comfortable. Little accidents don't disturb him. For tonight he will have the outhouse practically to himself. I've decided to spend the evening with some friends in a neighbouring village. As there is prospect of some fun, I give him the tip that I may not be home before morning. He receives the news without any perceptible trace of sorrow. Poor chap! he's to regret it before long.

Day has not yet dawned when I start on my return journey. I feel I should like a little sleep before the scrap. A sudden silence has sprung up all along the line, and I speed up to take advantage of this unaccustomed lull. But I have not yet reached home when the storm again breaks loose. The reason, of course, is obvious. All along the roads men are tramping to the trenches, to relieve those others who have been working for the past ten days. Fritz, naturally, is trying to thin their ranks.

*Crump! Crump! Crump!* So it goes all round. The day is breaking, and in the distance I see my billet. As I look, I see smoke. Lord! have they hit the house? I enter the yard, and the grey light reveals a heap of stones on the left. My room! I go nearer, to investigate the damage. Evidently the shell had hit the ground just outside, causing the wall on one side to collapse.

The corner where my bed stood has crumpled in. In the other, Scully's straw is lying undisturbed. I look round, wondering where he can be, and presently discover him amid the ruins. Poor chap! He had taken advantage of my tip to crawl into my more comfortable quarters. He has paid for the small pleasure with his life. But suppose I had been careful and stayed at home for the sake of my sleep? Well, evidently in this case the gods are rewarding the prodigal. Let us hope they will be equally kind on the morrow. Collins takes me in for the few hours remaining. By five I am out again to report to the Signal Office, where I am detailed to look after the wiring of a sector of trenches between two points north of Vermelles.

Already the activity of the artillery is so violent that the sky overhead resembles a sheet of steel. So thick and fast do the shells come that they seem a solid grey mass. Our ears are buzzing with the whir of their flight. Round us, too, explosions are sending up their spray of smoke. Our eyes begin to ache and our tongues have an acrid taste. Can a man preserve his mind amid such confusion of the senses?

I get my answer on entering the next traverse. This is the scene that meets my gaze: On the firing-step an altar has been erected. At it stands a Catholic priest. He is just finishing the morning mass. Round him on their knees are grouped a body of Irishmen,[1] caps in hand, their bent heads betraying the reverence in their hearts. By no sign, not even a side-glance at the havoc all round, do they show any interest in the peril of their position. Some faces are grim; all are grave, but not one shows a

---

1. Irish Regiments During the Great War by Michael MacDonagh also published by Leonaur.

trace of nervousness, much less of terror. For the moment they seem to be lifted by some super-human force above the physical horror of their surroundings.

And these are the same men who, a little later in the fight, are to quail before the torrent of the terrible liquid fire. Big, brawny and brave, they hesitated for a few seconds on the sight of this new instrument of torture. Then out rushed their commanding officer, waving their own flag.

"Up Irish, and at them!" he roared above the guns.

And with their war cry on their lips, they answered the challenge.

"*Fag a' bealach!*" they shouted, as they leapt forward to the attack, and though they fell like saplings under the sweep of a forest fire, the Germans had to yield before their fury.

"Wild beasts" was the name a Boche prisoner applied to them later, but there is no evidence of ferocity in them now. The mass over, they rise from their knees, shake themselves with a sigh, straighten up, and stroll off to their positions. Magnificent men, morally and physically, they can ill be spared by their small country, but of such war is reaping a heavy harvest.

It is 7:20. In ten minutes our artillery will lift the curtain and our men will go over the top. I am standing in a trench, directing some wiring, and incidentally watching the men who will make the fight. Territorials these, amateurs at the game, it is their first dip in the baptism of blood. It is curious to see how the different types react to the trial.

There is Charlie, who before the war was somebody's indifferent clerk with somewhat more energy than ability. When the first wave of patriotism struck his country, Charlie was on the top crest of the billow, bellowing with all his little might. An excitable gentleman, he is finding it hard to control his nerves. Now he sits on the firing step, grinning inanely. Now he walks up and down, cursing in a low tone. Presently a voice interrupts his soliloquy.

"Give us a match," say Bill, and the hand that takes it is steady. Bill is the calm cuss who enlisted as a matter of course, without enthusiasm, with no evidence of any ardour. Now he is smoking his pipe, but I notice that his eye wanders and always in the same direction, with an expression of anxiety and some sympathy. I follow his glance, and mine falls on Jim. He is sitting on the ground, white-faced but quiet. His sensitive features are positively twisted with terror, and between his lips hangs a cigarette that has been lit but is now dead.

"Have a light?" Bill says to him presently, and a mechanical smile lights up the fine face. Jim is one of those imaginative, highly strung lads who joined up from a sheer sense of duty, and who is seeing the thing through in a positive agony of fear.

"Up with you, boys," comes the order at last.

A quiver seems to run through the traverse, and instantly all the men are on their feet. Charlie makes for the firing-step with the uncertain gait of a blind man. Bill's walk is slow and deliberate. For a moment Jim holds back. Will the boy funk at the last lap? I can see the officer eyeing him, and again there is sympathy in the glance. But again his soul nerves him, though his heart fails. With a sudden rush, as if possessed by some demon of determination, the boy makes for the firing-step. Up he climbs, over the top, and is out ahead of the rest, the bravest man of the whole bunch.

5

Soon we are advancing at a rate which even the most optimistic would not have dared to hope for this morning. Trench after trench is taken by our men. We signallers are extending our lines forward. But the task becomes more difficult every moment. Shells, machine guns, even rifle fire are thinning our ranks, and at the same time cutting our cables. To keep the established communications intact and at the same time lay new lines would require double our usual complement of workers. We are already reduced to half.

But that is not our only problem. Elaborate systems of communication trenches had been dug to facilitate all movements of troops. Signboards stuck up all along the line gave direction in extreme detail.

"This way out!"

"This way in!"

"For the wounded."

They were all over the place, but no attention is being paid to them now. Every traverse is packed tight with the proverbial closeness of the sardine can. God! how the casualties are pouring in, in tens, twenties, fifties, hundreds. They lie on the ground; they line the walls. Sometimes so great is the congestion that new batches have to be borne out in the open, where an enemy shell occasionally mercifully puts them past their pain, or adds to it, as the case may be. And then the new men, the reinforcements on whom our hope depends to consolidate positions already won. They must be let through at all costs, and with the least possible exposure to danger.

Meantime in these very trenches our wires are being cut. How to get at them, and do the necessary repairing? Here and there a man manages to crawl through, but it takes so long, and we are already so handicapped! Out of twenty-six workers I have four left now. Request after request goes back for reinforcements. Finally they send me out twelve! But already complaints are coming in.

"See here, Mr. Signaller," one colonel says to me, "what the hell is the matter with our line? We can't distinguish a word that's being said. Better see to it. The telephone has gone groggy."

I look over it—D 3. It seems O.K. to me, but probably the line has been earthed somewhere. I send a lineman out to look for the cause of the trouble, and this is what he finds. I give the story, as he gave it to me.

"Well, Sir, I goes along the line and testin' every two 'undred yards, an' all of a suddint like I see a sight that makes me sick in my insides. Right there in front of me is sure enough 'Arry. Clearly, leastways, Sir, all that was left of 'im. 'E 'ad 'is left leg blown clean orf, Sir, and arf the other, and one bloomin' 'and orf, and gol-blimey, Sir, if 'e didn't 'ave the broken ends of the cable 'eld fast in 'is other 'and, and 'e stone dead, Sir.

"Well, Sir, I mends the cable and then looks abaht me, and I sees a long trail of blood abaht twenty yards. Poor 'Arry, Sir, 'e must 'ave been busted by a shell and then 'e crawled back, I suppose, Sir, with his arf a leg and arf an arm, and gripped the wire, Sir, and died."

There seems to be tears in Hawkins' voice as he tells the story. For a few moments he stops, looking at me indecisively, as if debating whether he shall proceed. Then he lowers his tone to a confidential pitch, as he goes on.

"You see, Sir, me and 'Arry was the best of pals. Sort of engaged to 'is sister, Lucy, I was, Sir. God Awmighty!" Of a sudden his pity gives way to fury, and a string of oaths and curses rain from his mouth. "I'll make those bleedin' swine pay for this, I will. You see if I don't." He has almost forgotten my presence. Then the rage subsides, and he sidles off, as if half ashamed. Poor fellow! he gets small chance to wreak the revenge he threatened. A piece of H.E. gets him a few hours later, and so I lose two of my most valuable men.

6

At last we have reached the quarries that lie between Hulluch and the Hohenzollern Redoubt. But it is a thin, tired line that now advances bravely on these formidable enemy defences, and yet a line on which our whole success depends. In the comparative security of the hollow behind these clay hills, the Boche has had time to steady himself. Now heavily re-enforced, he has rallied and is ready for the little troop that is so doggedly pressing on.

But why is the troop so little? What has become of the reserves that had been promised earlier from the 21st and 24th Divisions? Surely to heaven they won't fail us at a crisis like this when we had trusted to them for new strength in the terrible struggle?

On moves the line, and is met by the machine guns. It sways, steadies itself, sways again, falls back. Thicker and thicker comes the rain of bullets, pressing the advantage for the Boche. Again the line gives way—it is no more than a mere trickle now. Great God! won't those reserves ever come up?

Then a horrible thing happens to that tiny troop. It finds itself blocked from the rear. Barbed-wire, their own barbed-wire which the Engineers, sure of success, had moved too far up behind them! They attack it, try to tear it down, get entangled in their own efforts, a fine target for those terrible guns.

And still no sign of the reserves coming to the rescue!

What has happened? Who has blundered? Someone hints that the fault lies in the weakness of the cable communications. The hurried calls, they say, were delayed. The messages hadn't got through properly. I go hot and cold all over, as I listen. Surely to God they are telling lies. We couldn't have failed in spite of our efforts. They were desperate enough in all truth, and made against terrible odds. Well, if it is our fault, there is no use grumbling now. We can only stick to our posts and put our trust in the Scotchmen.

There they are out in front, putting up a desperate resistance—the London Scottish, first territorial regiment in the British army to make a charge. No one will dare to laugh at the "Terriers" after this. Time after time they rush at the oncoming Germans.

"Ladies from hell"[2] is the pretty compliment they earn from their enemy, in whose souls they are inspiring real terror.

Here is evidence of it close at hand—four hundred Boche prisoners sent to the rear after surrendering to one kiltie and three Royal Army Medical Corps men. They are trembling, poor chaps, and their faces are yellow with lyddite.

So it goes for days, attack and counter attack; trenches won and lost, now through gas, now through liquid fire. The expected reserves come at last, but too late. We had lost our great advantage. We had hampered the great advance. In one other part of the line an equal failure is reported, but it fails to afford us any consolation.

Then on October 8th the terrible battle is over. Comparative

---

2. *Ladies From Hell,* by R. Douglas Pinkerton also published by Leonaur.

quiet reigns along the line. We proceed to a counting of our casualties. Sixty thousand in two weeks. There was never a war like this war. But the Germans are even worse off than we. Eighty *per cent.*, something over 100,000 men! Well, I can rival them in my small way. Out of a unit of fifty, I have lost forty men, and every one of them killed.

Well, as I have said, we are now enjoying a comparative calm, and I am now on another part of the line. In the fighting to the South round Loos and facing Hill 70, we have lost a brigade signal officer, and I am detailed to his post. I find the office in a disused house to the east of the village, about a mile and a half away from the famous hill.

Again there is a deadlock along the front, and I proceed to get my section into working order. There is plenty to be done these days in the way of repairing. Occasionally Fritz disturbs us at the job. He sends over a shell by way of reminder that he is not yet *hors de combat*, and at times succeeds in putting us in that condition.

About a week after I had taken on my new job, I was sitting at my desk in the Signal Office, a much more elaborate affair than the farmhouse kitchen in which I found myself at the start. This is a large, long room. At one end and along one side is a bench to which telegraph and buzzer instruments are attached. At these sit the operators working. On the other side is a switchboard with its attendant. In the centre at a desk—to be accurate, a large box—sits the sergeant, supervisor of the slaves. Behind him at another desk—an inferior box—are two corporals, one acting as despatch clerk, and the other as checking clerk, whose duty it is to keep tabs on all messages, whether incoming or outgoing.

Well, on the day when Fritz decided to get busy, we were all at our posts—more's the pity. For some time the artillery had been exchanging compliments, but to these we paid no attention. It was a habit of theirs, and had never yet disturbed us. However, one never knows along the line. This time, it seems, our turn had come.

Straight through the roof, with a horrible crash, tore a shell, splitting the house in half. For a moment the noise stunned me, and I was thrown out of my chair right on the top of the orderly who was sharing my corner. Then I stood up and looked round, to find myself *al fresco*. It was one of the strangest freak shots that I have ever seen. Gone were all the instruments with their operators. Gone, too, were the sergeant and the two corporals. And here were the orderly and myself, standing safely in the shaky remnant of the room. These, I might add, are the little accidents that shake a man's nerve. At times, however, they serve to strengthen a man's belief in his luck, give him the impression that he is somehow immune. But let me tell you another story that came to my notice next day, and gave me pause in my rejoicing over my escape.

There was a widow in the North of England who had five sons before the war. One was a regular soldier. He went to France in August, 1914. His brothers, civilians before, now joined Kitchener's Army and went out with the first hundred thousand.

Now Bill, as we call the regular—I've heard but forgotten his name—was in every scrap going from the start. He fought at Mons, on the Marne, at the Aisne, Neuve Chapelle, and just now he had come safely through Loos. The other four had not lasted more than a few days on the line. They were killed, one after the other.

Now the War Office, though a machine, betrays human feeling at times. On this occasion it was moved by the tale of the five brothers and the mother they had left alone in the North of England. So the order, after much red tape, went forth to the front to release Bill and send him home to a profitable job at munition making, where he could help his country and his mother in comparative immunity from death.

So Bill, who had just survived the slaughter at Loos, packed his kit without regrets, shook hands with his friends and mounted the motor lorry that was to take him to the station. You might think that the immortals had no use for Bill, having let him live so long in the midst of death. But Mars, it seems, must have his little joke.

He was in sight of the station and of safety, one would say, when overcame a shell, picked the motor lorry for a target, and up it went, carrying Bill to Kingdom Come.

It was a sour-faced sergeant who told me the tale. It was most effective in shaking my belief in my own immunity. I presume that was his object in telling it. As the American cartoonist says, "*Someone is always taking the joy out of life.*"

7

Here we are again, going up in the world all the time. Now myself and my orderly, with our new instruments and our new operators are installed in no meaner quarters than a *château!* They've given us the dining-room. I believe my maps are spread on the very table at which fair ladies of France once sat and sipped champagne. *Sic transit*, says the poet. The glory of goblets is replaced by charts. Still they are helping to save the ladies' country.

Nothing exciting so far, save Fritz's morning frolics. The blighter is always disturbing our best sleep. Never mind! We've *upset one of his apple-carts today*. He is not quite as efficient as he thinks he is, at least, when it comes to learning our language. Apt to be too accurate—which is a mistake.

Only today Sergeant-Major Bradley of our Signal Section was strolling through one of the village streets. As he passed, he noticed a man near the top of one of those odd-looking towers which in France take the place of the telephone poles used in this country. Now the sergeant-major happens to be in charge of our linemen. He knows every one of them not only by sight but by name; moreover, he has an accurate memory for the duties he has told them to do. He failed to remember, however, that any man had been assigned to that tower. Then what the devil was he doing up there, testing the wires? This, at a casual glance, seemed to be the gentleman's occupation.

The sergeant-major who had passed decided to retrace his

steps and investigate. With certain omissions which you can supply for yourself, he shouted to the figure on high.

"What ———— are you doing there? Who ———— are you, anyway?"

"I'm a Royal Engineer," came the answer.

Now, as it happens, no seasoned member of our corps ever refers to himself by such a title. He might call himself an R.E., though that is unusual. He prefers either "sapper" or "lineman"

"Oh, indeed!" said the sergeant, becoming facetious. "Royal Engineer, are ye? Well, suppose you come down and let's have a look at ye."

The man prepared to descend. There was nothing else to do, but as he complied with the request he slipped something in his pocket, which did not fail to catch the wary sergeant's eye.

"So you're a Royal Engineer," he reiterated, when the gentleman had reached the ground. "And what might this be?"

Putting his hand in the man's pocket he drew out a neat leather case. It was a most compact instrument for tapping the wires.

That man was in his grave before two hours, and the sergeant is likely to wear a decoration.

# CHAPTER 4

# In Which the Wireless Comes Into Its Own on the British Front

### 1

It was during the Battle of Loos that some gentleman entitled to think—only important people have that privilege in the army—decided it was high time that the British forces took advantage of Mr. Marconi's invention. True, wireless had not been unknown in the world military. Indeed its introduction there practically coincided with its *début* in civil life. But so far the appointed controllers of the Signal Service destinies had looked on the interloper with disfavour. They preferred the time-honoured method of the regular telephone, which had weathered so many a test, but which, alas! collapsed so often in a crisis.

Our friend Fritz, on the contrary, had shown no such tender prejudice. Always the leader in military fashions, he had been using the wireless telephone from the very start in his communications, and always presumably with excellent results. Wherefore it was decreed to offer him the delicate compliment—than which there is none more delicate or sincere—of imitating him in this particular line.

So at Loos we started—also with excellent results. Whence hangs the rest of our tale. Justified by the experiment, the aforesaid gentleman or his friends decided to elaborate and extend the new system, thereby initiating a minor revolution in the methods of the Royal Engineer Signal Service.

Immediately there went forth a call for qualified men for the work. Post offices, private wireless companies, telegraph offices were combed for operators already familiar with the intricacies of the Morse code or the rudiments of the more necessary radio work. The small schools which had formerly turned out the insignificant body of army operators were enlarged beyond all expectation. A new curriculum was chosen, and a new standard set, calling for very definite and very high qualifications on the part of the graduates.

The new army operator had to be able to send and receive the Morse code at the rate of twenty-five words a minute English or twenty words code and foreign languages. As a matter of fact, fifteen was about as rapid as he could use, though he might need twenty in times of particular stress. No chances, however, were taken in the matter of speed. Then he had to be able to assemble and dismantle a standard Marconi set. He had to be able to hoist and strike steel aerial poles. He had to have a working knowledge of a trench set and a thorough knowledge of army procedure.

This course took him anywhere from two to three months to cover, according to his native ability and the extent of his previous knowledge. That knowledge, indeed, was usually small, for the average Englishman had seldom indulged in these semi-scientific studies. His American cousin, with his natural aptitude for these abstruse subjects, is far ahead of him here. Indeed, judging by a short but close connection with radio sections of the American army which I have had since my advent in the United States, I should be inclined to predict that in this branch of the service the American boy will beat all comers.

Still, allowing for this general innate disinclination—few Britishers would not prefer a bayonet to a wireless box—our schools did rapid and efficient work. Soon qualified men were pouring over to France. Meantime behind the firing line we were preparing officers to receive them. All Signal officers who could be spared from brigade and division headquarters and who, of course, were already familiar with telegraphy and circuits, were sent behind the line for a three-weeks' course which would give them sufficient knowledge of the work to enable them to command a radio section, until regular radio officers were ready to take their places. And every officer on the line who showed any knowledge of wireless was brought back to act as instructor in the new schools.

During my short stay at the depot in England, I had confessed in an incautious moment to having done some wireless work in school. Now I was to reap the consequences of my indiscretion—in the army, as in the law courts, everything you say can be used against you. Besides, I was still a Cook's tourist, with no fixed abiding place, so presently I found myself departing from my small command with a ticket for General Headquarters way back beyond the line. St. Omer was the nearest station, but my billet was at Roquetoire in a *château* which housed the school as well as the scholars.

Here our work was conducted with that apparent absence of effort which seems to characterise all activities in the environment of the High Command. In the morning we went on excursions, always carrying our little wireless sets with which we experimented in the pleasantest spots to be found in the surrounding country. Or we had rather informal discussions on elementary electrical subjects which were never prolonged beyond three-thirty in the afternoon. After that hour our time was our own, to be disposed of according to our inclinations. Were it not for the omnipresence of certain red-tabbed gentlemen in whose presence discreet behaviour was advisable, this period might have marked a highwater mark in the way of amusements.

St. Omer was a pleasant place, and quite close when one possessed a motor-cycle. But those red-tabbed gentlemen and the generals they surrounded were very numerous on its crooked old streets, too numerous from the point of view of a mere subaltern. Still one can't expect unalloyed delights. At least the guns were far distant. They no longer disturbed our sleep. And the beds boasted clean linen, and there was hot water for our baths.

And we ate our meals off a dining table, and never extracted them from a can. Indeed, on the whole, we had reason to be grateful to the gentleman above mentioned who not only possessed but used his privilege of individual thought.

## 2

It was not long before the wireless system, developing with that miraculous rapidity which characterises all developments in a modern fighting army, had established itself as an important, not to say indispensable, part of every section of the British forces in France. In the trenches, with the guns, on the aeroplanes, at headquarters—in short, everywhere, the radio had its definite place and different form according to the exigencies of the position assigned to it.

During the great retreat its role with the infantry was practically monopolised by a few motor lorry sets which, though small, had played a significant part. To the casual observer these are no more than ordinary trucks, the bodies of which are limited by the small space of twelve feet by six. As a matter of fact, they are extraordinarily compact and ingenious contrivances, an entrance to which is effected from the rear. Looking in from here, one sees at the far end a bench about three feet high by four feet deep, above and below which are placed complicated instruments, recognisable only to the initiated.

Along the sides of the truck run lockers about eighteen inches high by eighteen deep in which are neatly stowed various poles of various lengths to be taken out as occasion requires. Underneath the truck is stored another set of these poles, for this can be used either as a mobile or fixed station, and different requirements demand different apparatus.

One might imagine that all this paraphernalia would take up all the small available space. Not so, however. There were still two operators to fit in, one for receiving and transmitting the messages, the other for logging, filing and distributing. This latter function was discharged usually by orderlies, four or five of whom as a rule followed outside on bicycles. Whenever a message had to be delivered to a commanding officer within the truck's sector, one of these men rode off with it—a very easy job compared with that of the men inside the truck.

Quiet, you know, is considered essential for an operator's work as a rule, but quiet was the last thing these operators could hope to have. To being with, there was the incessant noise from the automobile engine; then there was the continual bumping over the uneven French roads; lastly, there was the roar of the guns in the distance, and not the dim distance, either, very often.

There was an operator once whose truck was hit by a shell. A flying splinter from the wagon caught him in the foot, but he stuck to his job, though in terrible pain. How could he leave it, with no relief nearby? I don't know how long it was before that relief finally came; but there was another man whose relief failed him for some thirty-nine hours. From seven o'clock one morning until ten the next night he sat in his wagon, in his horribly cramped position, never taking the 'phones from his ears. A superman, if you will. There were many of them in those days, the early days, the dark days, when one man did the work of many, when we were fighting an army of fully-equipped millions with only thousands to hold them off—days that are gone, thank heaven, for good!

But to come back to our motor lorry wireless sets. With the finish of the moving fighting they went temporarily out of use. Trench wireless apparatus became the great need now. The old telephone was good, but so long as communications depended on cable that a chance shell might at any moment cut, so long were the communications undependable and therefore dangerous.

A portable wireless for front line use that a single man could carry, that would not be a tempting target for machine gun fire, that would be not easily disabled even by the bursting of a shell—that was the instrument which the experimenters aimed at. And it was evolved by slow degrees. In its final form—which it did not assume till some months later—it consisted of a box eighteen inches by nine, weighing just fifteen pounds and having a range easily of five miles.

I remember when the first experiments were made with this set, some distance back of the line. They took the form of contests between the wireless and the old telephone. A detachment of each would start off from a trench, as if during an actual engagement, to a position some five hundred yards off. Then each would do his utmost to establish communications in the shortest possible time. The men, being on their mettle, did their best. But from the first the wireless man won, usually by an average of some thirty seconds—no small consideration in actual warfare, when perhaps it is a question of holding conquered ground against strong resistance.

The instrument being thus perfected and the operators trained, the wireless telephone took its place on the line. Now when the Tommy advances to an attack, there is always a radio man somewhere in the rear. Where formerly a detachment had to reel out hundreds and hundreds of yards of cable to establish telephonic communication between the new positions and the old, now an operator picks up his box and his aerial, and advances simultaneously with the attackers. Arrived he crouches in a nearby crater, throws out his aerials along the ground, and establishes communications forthwith. The infantry is gaining. He follows right along. The infantry is retreating. He beats it back behind them. So has the wireless simplified matters along the line.

With the air service it is, naturally, of infinitely more importance. Here, however, it was always in use, being essential to the success of the work. The aviator has been called the "eyes of the army," but if those eyes lacked a mouth through which to tell what they have seen, they would often be just as useful if blindfold.

Suppose a "spotter" has gone up to locate an enemy battery that has been creating havoc along our line. Suppose he locates it—a difficult business in these days of effective camouflage. Naturally it is out of sight both for our guns and their Forward Observation Officers. It is the "spotter's" business then to give our artillery the range and direct their fire. This he does by means of his wireless apparatus. Having given them the approximate distance, he signals down:

"Go."

They fire. It is a cloudy day, and they use high explosive which, giving out a yellowish puff, is undistinguishable to an airman's eye. Back he signals:

"Shrapnel."

This gives out a white cloud of smoke. They fire again. He sees it, but the shot goes over the target and a couple of hundred yards to the right. By means of a code he tells them the approximate distance by which they have missed. They fire again. Somewhat nearer, but not yet right. He signals again. They shift their range according to his instructions. So it continues until, finally, he flashes the letter:

"Z."

In artillery parlance, they have "hit."

And this is only one detail of the work the air wireless does. It is invaluable for the aviator's operations. But we have not yet reached the end of the radio's activities.

Back at army headquarters, where enemy shells do not often fall, the aerial raises a high and honoured head. Here is situated a large Marconi station, the chief duties of which are the intercepting of enemy communications and the taking of aircraft reports. With this, too, are connected smaller sets at Brigade, and so on up to the trenches, where they ultimately get in touch with our tiny portable boxes. Thus does wireless as well as cable telephone link up the whole line.

There was a captious gentleman once who complained that much activity was wasted by this chain of ever greater sets of wireless apparatus. Why not, he asked, replace them all by one large set close to the line which could link them all up at once with general headquarters in the rear? Much time, he argued, could thus be saved.

His suggestion was adopted. I remember the occasion quite distinctly. The station was erected. It consisted of a motor lorry set, 1½ K.W., a 120-foot steel mast, an umbrella aerial, with a complement of three operators. For two hours it reared its un-diminished head. Then over came one of those unsanctified 5.9 shells, and presently we were witnessing the ungodly sight of the lorry set, the steel mast, the umbrella aerial and the three operators being shot skyward to various points of the compass. Presumably they have descended since, but I saw no evidences of their fall. They were scattered too far and wide to leave any traces.

Thus was the captious gentleman answered out of the mouth of the enemy guns. So we resumed our tiresome chain of ever larger wireless sets, and saved ourselves much expense and many lives.

3

The fickle masters of my destiny suddenly deciding that I had rested sufficiently long at Roquetoire, I was soon taking a hasty and none too reluctant farewell of that village and its many red-tabbed visitors. My orders were to proceed south to a brigade situated somewhere near Albert. I set out under a glorious sky on a very good road, and my instructions allowing some elastic-ity of interpretation in the matter of time, I made no haste to reach the scene of unpleasant action. The theatre of war had no attractions for me now. The set pieces had gone stale, and such surprises as it staged at times were not of a nature calculated to allure. At St. Pol, an old stamping ground, I delayed till the last minute. But soon the seventy-odd miles that separated me from my station had sped by under the smooth wheels of my all-too-swift car.

So here I am again, Supernumerary Signal Officer still at-tached to a unit that I may not claim as my own. Oh, the joys of the tourist *à la Cook!* I am to assist the brigade signal officer with the telephonic communications. But as these consist mainly in superintending the wiring of places that are very seldom shelled and more seldom hit, or the receiving of messages concerning the company's foot- and under-wear, I am liable to have much leisure on my hands. My masters, however, have foreseen such a contingency and duly forestalled any designs that His Satanic Majesty might have had on my idle hands. Our radio system being still far from perfect, I am to devote my odd moments to experimentation with the same. Those odd moments are more easily counted as hours. The Boche is behaving with extraordinary restraint, and we are most carefully doing nothing to provoke his sleeping wrath.

To one accustomed to a war atmosphere blue with smoke and shrill with screams, there is something uncanny in the calm monotony that characterises activities down here. There is the same routine in the trenches so far as the Tommies are concerned. Four days in billets, four along the line, rising at "Stand-to" in the dim, grey dawn, filling sandbags, cleaning rifles, taking a turn at listening post. An occasional excursion across No Man's Land when the night is dark and the enemy quietly at rest stirs the blood and makes a break in the monotony, but even these sallies rarely result in a real scrap. The object is rather to avoid such a clash, and the hope merely to take some unwary prisoner from whom we may elicit information regarding his superior's plans. For the rest, there is the waiting, endless, hopeless. For what? Heaven only knows.

Poker proves a preventive for many a fit of the blues. Cursing is the safety-valve, if the fit gets fastened on one. There is some desultory betting on the direction of the shells between gamblers whom the chance of being hit does not even excite.

"Bet you the next one gets that ole stump," challenges Jones.

His chum, as a kindness, takes him on.

"Bet you it 'its the 'eap of stones."

But so long has one to wait for it to hit anywhere that the bet is all but forgotten when it falls.

Some men of more domestic—or more greedy—natures, turn their attention to the inner man. In my strolls through the trenches I come on some of these venturesome people trying to vary the monotony of bully beef by devices learned, presumably, from nature herself. A little strategy and foresight exerted when in billets provides the wherewithal for the experiments.

When one knows how to handle *Madame*, the redoubtable, the parsimonious, one may gather such luxuries as potatoes or eggs with which to swell the regular larder. For instance, a sack of the former may be extracted as the price for cutting up her stock of precious wood, or mending her windows removed suddenly by a shell, or finding tarpaulin to cover the airholes in her roof. And with potatoes one may concoct that delectable dish known on the line as "cottage pie."

A layer of bully chopped fine, overlaid by a layer of potatoes mashed to a pulp, the whole baked in a mess tin over a fire-bucket—that is a recipe to be relished by any "regular." It was the smell of it that lured an unlucky private one day from his traverse into a neighbouring one where it was cooking. It was dinner hour—12 a.m.—in the trenches. His meal was the bully and biscuits cold, so he decided, evidently, to "cadge," if he could.

"Cottage pie, 'ave ye?" he said, casually strolling up to the six fortunate Tommies who were sitting round their fire-bucket, devouring it. "My eye, but some blokes is lucky. "Where did ye get the spuds'?"

"Back in billets, ole dear." A long pause through which the visitor waited patiently. "'Ave a bit." It came at last, with reluctance. People should provide their own luxuries or do without. The tardiness of the invitation, however, in no wise discouraged the intruder.

"Ah don't mind if ah do," he decided, sitting down.

A long silence, broken only by such sounds as are not prescribed in the books of etiquette to accompany a man's meals. Then suddenly the silences were broken—the Boche chooses unfortunate times to get busy. There was a prolonged *hiss* quite close to the ear, a *bang*, followed by a cloud of smoke, and up spattered the earth over our seven silent friends, covering them with stray bits of mud. A "pip-squeak" had hit the trench.

In a second it was all over. Recovering, they looked round.

And at the end of the traverse they saw the visitor lying sidewise, a mess tin still clutched in his hands.

"Got 'is," commented one man, who had gone to turn him over.

"Why the 'ell didn't 'e stay where he belonged?"

Even with a surplus on our hands, we waste no time on sentimentality. Callousness does not necessarily decrease with the size of the casualty list. Ours is a very small one indeed. For days not a single case will come into the casualty clearing station, a happy change from those times when we had sixty thousand in less than a week. Sometimes it is the Boche laxity and sometimes a lucky chance that saves the life on our side. One day, suffering, I suppose, from a sudden attack of the old hate, the gentleman sent two hundred and eighty shells flying into the little village of Bienvillers, which is a few kilos away from our quarters. And not a single soul did he send to heaven.

But another evening he hurled a "big Bertha," just one solitary piece of explosive, right into the middle of the square. He timed it and aimed it well, for we were holding a band concert at the moment, and all the happy, harmless villagers were disporting themselves in the open. Thirty dead and more wounded was the toll that shell took! Such are the unpleasant surprises on the line.

But on the whole we have no reason to complain, for which we have to thank our friends, the Saxons. They, we are assured on good authority, are our opponents on this particular part of the line, an amiable race, judging from their attitude towards us. We ascribe those sudden fits of temper to the arrival of visiting Prussian officers, grim gentlemen with a fondness for fireworks.

4

Meantime we are discovering the virtues and vices of our new radio system of communications. We had begun by using a perpendicular aerial which stuck its head rather too prominently over the parapet, thereby incurring all the hardships and hazards that had made life insecure for our old cable. Occasionally it stood for days, but this was due to the Boche indifference. When they woke up, its short span was measured in minutes. A most undependable contrivance, but we had taken no risks with it as yet, and we had leisure to look for a substitute. This was presently evolved in the form of ground aerials that, lying along the earth, were practically indistinguishable and therefore as safe a system as could be found.

A very excellent thing, indeed, we found Mr. Marconi's invention, when adapted to our peculiar requirements. Its chief charm, of course, lay in its extreme simplicity, a quality which, unfortunately, acted as a boomerang at times. Put it in the hands of an experienced gentleman operating behind our lines, with the object not of helping but of hindering us, and its charm took on a different aspect. There were many of these gentlemen in the old days in France. Most ingenious and elusive people they proved to be. Disturbing stories of their versatility used to float towards us at times, borne on those strange news currents that spring up along the line. Positive genius characterises some of their activities. The palm in this particular goes, I think, to the individual whose tale I am now going to tell.

There was a subaltern on our side, a youngster just "out," who was suffering from a bad attack of souvenir mania. The malady being rather general, he was forever in danger of having a curio pinched from his collection. Consequently, when he became possessed of a Boche rifle and bayonet, he made haste to put it in safe hiding. For this purpose he chose the chimney of his billet bedroom. Whence hangs the thread of this tale.

Putting his hand up the chimney to find a resting place for the butt of his rifle, he was surprised to find it touching a pole of bamboo. He pulled; the pole came; then stuck, and no pulling could bring it any farther. Being curious by nature as well as by training, he determined to investigate—which led him to the roof.

It was a typical roof of a French provincial house, flat, with a chimney protruding at each end and a slight elevation of the wall above the gutter. The first thing to catch his eye when he reached it was a set of wires lying close to the surface. One ran from chimney to chimney. It was an open wire. The other which was insulated, adjoined this at right angles at the centre and ran toward the side of the house. The first wire, he found on closer inspection, stretched not only up to but into the chimney, running up its side in a neatly made groove. He gave it a tug, and up came a bamboo pole.

It took very few seconds for him to reach the street. He was young and extremely excited. He was in a hurry to find somebody in authority to whom he might report, and by good luck came on a staff officer walking through the town.

"I wonder if you could give me a moment, Sir," he began breathlessly saluting, "to come up to my roof. There's dirty work, I think, Sir, being done there."

"Oh!" said the red-tabbed one, not particularly excited. He had heard such breathless tales before. "And what might it be?"

"An aerial, Sir, so far as I can judge."

"Good lud! Come along. Let's have a look."

They went off together, and were presently on the roof.

"You're right, sonny," said the officer after a few seconds' inspection. "That's what it is. I wonder where's the rest? Now you follow that wire," he pointed to the one that was insulated. "That's the feeding wire for this aerial, I should say."

The boy set to work. He found that the wire entered a drain at the back of the house, reappeared at the bottom, then vanished through the wall. So far it was easy, but no rummaging seemed to unearth the rest. Where the dickens was the instrument! Finally he decided that there was nothing for it but to dig through. This process performed, he found himself in a cellar and also at the end of his search. For here, buried deep under a pile of dirt and straw, was a very neat, very complete German wireless apparatus. It was even equipped with a zinc box round the spark gap to prevent any crackling of the transmissions being heard.

"Hm-m-m," said the staff officer, "and who the devil works

this? Run and fetch me *Monsieur*—Whatdyecallem the owner of your billet, my boy."

After twenty minutes' search the boy returned.

"Can't find him, Sir, and no one seems to know where he has gone. They're so stupid. Don't seem to understand me."

So far as I know, no one has found him since. He was a short, stocky gentleman with a bullet head and shrewd eyes. Contrary to all custom, it was now remembered he had offered no objections to excuses when they requisitioned his house—the best in the town and therefore the obvious billet for the officers. On the contrary, he had always exerted himself to make his guests cosy and comfortable. Though unobtrusive, he had been exceedingly attentive—which, perhaps, ought to have aroused suspicion. How he ever managed to hoist the aerial remains a mystery to this day. Probably he climbed out of his attic at dusk, when the officers were at the mess, dining. But that is only guess-work. The rest is fact.

<br>

5

And now we are nearing our second Christmas, a season that may be merry or very miserable. Holidays, bringing their reminder of a lapse in old associations, are apt to be depressing on the line. Last year we celebrated with a twenty-four hour truce. This year there is to be no such official recognition of the meaning of the great festival. Truces are inclined to be trying on the morale, particularly when accompanied by fraternisation between the opposing forces. On the other hand, we must do something to mark the day, and the onus of the occasion lies, of course, on the officers. It has already become a custom for them to assume the duty of enlivening and otherwise cheering the men. Life here being in the raw, divested of all semblance of luxury, the efforts of the officers are particularly directed to the procuring of creature comforts.

For weeks before, the campaign is on. It takes the form of correspondence. Relatives and friends once forgotten recur pleasantly to mind, particularly those possessed of generous souls. Casual little postscripts convey delicate little hints. Details are forwarded on request and after that—the deluge. Canned, tinned, bottled, boxed—all the forms and varieties of food and drink that can be safely entrusted to the sea, come pouring over to the brigade. My billet is picked out as storehouse, for the simple reason that I live there by myself, and seem to have more room than the rest. I say "seem" advisedly. As a matter of fact, it is very small, and besides me and my batman, it houses the old owner and his wife. However, we are willing to bark our shins against the boxes and risk breaking our necks by tripping over hampers down the stairs. What's a leg more or less in such a cause! Fritz, however, is not disposed to be so friendly. Which leads me to perhaps the saddest of all the sad incidents I witnessed during my time at the front.

The old couple with whom I lived—they were both over seventy—had already suffered more than their due share in the war. But with a persistence peculiar to the French peasant, they refused to move farther behind the line. They preferred to stay with their old home, damaged as it was, and their stock which had been reduced to one cow and a pig. Before the outbreak they had been happy, and looked forward to an old age, provided for by three sturdy sons. These had gone, and had died. But the old couple did not complain. They just looked stricken. They were sad, but very quiet, and they tended very faithfully to all my wants.

One morning I went off to a neighbouring town, where I stayed until late afternoon. When I returned it was to find the old lady sitting in the ruins of her home, groaning and rocking herself to and fro. Some neighbours were with her, but she paid no attention to their sympathy. Seeing me, however, she sprang to her feet, and before I could stop her, she had thrown herself on the ground at my feet.

"For God's sake go and kill them! Kill the cursed Boches!" Her voice rose to a shrill scream, and she wound her arms around my ankles. "Look at what they've done to me. Oh, won't you go and kill them!" She was quite beside herself with grief.

We did our best to calm her, and by and by she quieted clown. Then she told me what had happened. She had gone out to do her marketing, leaving the old man in charge. When she came back, it was to find him killed, her stock blown to atoms, and her house apparently split in two. A couple of shells had pitched close to it. So here she was at seventy, without kin, cattle or money.

Her home, however, proved not to be absolutely beyond repair, judged by the standards that hold along the front. Tarpaulin and ground sheets manipulated by the Tommies made it weatherproof, and we continued to live in it. Our store of food, fortunately enough, was not much damaged.

But this was not the only accident that threatened our Christmas preparations. Another, not quite so serious, eventuated a little later. According to custom, also, the officers had raked together some few pounds to be spent on the spot. Our brigade being averse to unnecessary labour, the disposing of the money was put in the hands of the sergeant, who in turn left the decision to the men.

Their taste ran to pork, so a pig was procured, one of those long-legged, lean but sleek and satisfying animals that are so much favoured in France. For weeks before Christmas this precious brute came in for more attention than he had ever received in his life. It is surprising that he did not die of overfeeding. Probably his activity saved him, for he was extremely active, as we had reason to regret later.

Then two days before the holiday rose the all-important question: Who was going to kill old Aristophe? You see, we had even christened him, so much did we care for him. As a rule there are few trades unrepresented in a platoon, but ours did not boast of a pig-sticker. It was a terrible moment, when the men made this discovery. Yet none seemed willing to undertake the necessary task. Killing Boches was one thing, but killing pigs was quite another. Everyone seemed to shrink from the encounter. And then—heaven can be kind—someone suggested finding a friend, a Connaught man now connected with the Army Service Corps, who had once practised the unpleasant trade in the West of Ireland.

But would he come? They put it up to him. He agreed on one condition—that he be allowed to share the excellent Christmas dinner. No one had thought of arranging festivities for the non-combatants of the A.S.C. Needless to say, the bargain was struck on the spot, and arrangements made for the ceremony of execution.

Perhaps you have seen pigs killed and know all the terrible details. I hadn't, neither had the other officers. So we all gathered round, while the sturdy man from Mayo tied three of the animal's legs, drew the rope through a ring, which, fixed in the wall close to the ground, was intended to keep him steady. Then, stretched on his back with the other leg kicking freely—this so that he might pump out his own precious lifeblood—he was ready for the thrust of the knife. Perhaps our presence had made the hangman's hand unsteady, or perhaps he wasn't really a pig-sticker, and had only pretended to be one for the sake of the meal.

Anyway, he had just inserted the deadly weapon in the animal's throat, when up flew the three tied legs. Neatly, so neatly that even a boxer could not do it better, he sent a punch home on the executioner's jaw. Down went the Mayo man sprawling on the earth, and off ran the victim, his blood streaming behind him.

Straight through the village street he sped, pursued by the whole brigade, privates, non-coms., subalterns and colonels. And then—crowning coup on his part—he headed straight for the enemy's line. Were we to resign him to Fritz, or would we risk our heads for the sake of the dinner? Fortunately we were saved such an alternative. That indecisive knife-thrust was doing its deadly work—the track of red which we were following told that. Presently, after covering some eight or nine hundred yards, he fell, limp from loss of blood. And so the men had pork as the *pièce de resistance*. But the Connaught man came in for some sarcasm all the same.

But though Christmas preparations might amuse us in our leisure, they were not allowed to divert us from our labour. Experiments were still going forward, but mine were now being conducted under the earth. To procure the necessary isolation and tranquillity, a sort of subterranean workshop had been dug. It consisted of a gallery ten feet long by six high, situated about eighteen feet beneath the surface. You entered this through a sap, that is a tunnel, four feet in diameter, through which you crawled on hands and knees. This sap ran at right angles to the bottom of a communication trench connecting two support trenches, probably the loneliest position that could be procured along the line. Even at the busiest times these communication trenches are quiet places, disturbed only by a passing foot.

No place, however, could be too quiet for us. It was for this reason that I decided to work on Christmas Eve. Then every man not absolutely essential to the manning of the front line would be released for the purpose of amusing himself. Then, too, the Boche, so surprisingly innocuous even in his most dangerous moments, might be counted on to devote himself to his carols. So I notified my assistants, a corporal named Blackmore and a private named Weston, to meet me at midnight on December 24th at the mouth of our solitary sap.

It was a damp, cold night, but nobody was minding the weather. By nine the festivities were in full swing. The mess-halls were merry with the clink of glasses. From the huts resounded the roar of lusty throats. I peeped in at one company concert, and found the stage occupied by perhaps the most disreputable figure I have ever beheld at the front. His boots were muddy; his *puttees* drooped disconsolately, and his tunic looked as if it had been dragged through a bramble bush. But the music that he wrung from the company piano would make even Kitchener himself overlook greater faults than these.

Before I left, his place was taken by a perky little Cockney, who "rendered": "Just a little love, a little kiss," in a voice calculated to draw tears from a turnip. He had just prepared himself, as shown by the sentimental break in his voice, to give adequate expression to the words, "I love you," when from the back of the hall, sung to the air of the song, came a ribald roar:

"Golblimey."

I departed, followed by the shouts of laughter from which even the officers in attendance could not refrain. I never learned how the Cockney took the interruption. Then, having imbibed a tonic suitable to the state of the weather, I went off to join my men.

7

It was exactly midnight as we bent to enter our sap. Blackmore and I went in first.

"Not a soul in sight," he said, as we descended. "Thank God, there won't be anyone to disturb us." And he was right. We were to recall his remark later.

We two had just connected up our instruments, when Weston, coming in from the mouth of the tunnel, reported the Boches as becoming unusually busy. Barely were the words out of his mouth, when the ground quivered all round us. There came a shower of mud and dirt from the top of the gallery. We heard an explosion, a loud rumble, followed immediately by a deep thud and a back draught of air that blew out our solitary candle.

"What the devil—?" began Blackmore.

We lit up again, went along the gallery into the sap to see what had happened, and found our passage blocked by a solid wall of earth. We looked at one another stupidly. There was dead silence for a few moments. It was Weston who finally spoke first.

"Let's dig the stuff away," he said, "before we begin work."

I noticed there was a quiver in his voice.

Without comment, however, we all set to dig. I looked at my watch. The time was 12:17. Our only tools were two jack-knives and my revolver. Dig, dig, dig—we went at it nervously, earnestly, absolutely in silence. After a while I looked at my watch again, expecting to see that an hour had passed. It was exactly 12:22. Half involuntarily I stop work, and the others follow my example. We all sit down on the earth. So far we have avoided even meeting each other's eyes. Now we look at one another cautiously, probingly, trying not to betray our own knowledge of the position we are placed in. Quite obviously there are thirty-five feet of solid earth to be shovelled away before we can get out into that support trench. Quite probably that, too, is blocked by crumbled clay. The shell may have blown the parapets down on both sides. There is not the slightest chance that a man will pass anywhere near us tonight. Possibly none will pass even to-morrow.

"Let's shout," says Weston.

A perfectly futile suggestion, but we welcome it. It means something to do. Simultaneously and individually we scream at the tops of our voices, but all the answer we get is the echo. The louder our shouts, the greater the reverberation in our ears. But we keep it up, until our throats are dry and hoarse.

"I'll try my revolver," I say to break the silence.

I fire one shot, and the sound reflected from the walls of the gallery almost splits the drums of our ears. But even that seems better than a flat acknowledgment of failure. One after another I shoot all six rounds. Our ears are aching, and our heads buzzing from the noise. When I have finished, we sit a while in silence, as if expecting some answer. But none comes, of course. That was a foregone conclusion.

"Well, there is nothing for it but to dig. Once again we go at it. Tiny handfuls of earth falling at our feet reward our efforts— strenuous efforts that cause the perspiration to pour from our faces. So concentrated is my attention of the particular task in hand that I lose consciousness entirely of my comrades, until suddenly my attention is attracted by a strange noise from behind. I turn. There is Weston squatting on the ground, singing in a silly, soft voice to himself.

"What the devil is he up to?" I asked Blackmore, testily.

"Loony," comes the brief reply.

"Loony?" I repeat the word stupidly after him.

"Yes, potty, you know—gone off his nut." He makes the announcement calmly, to be taken as a matter of course.

Lord! what a pretty pickle we're in! Suppose I should come to that? It makes me shiver. I look at Blackmore, white-faced, steady-eyed, silent. He meets my eye, smiles, shrugs his shoulders. I smile back. Fine chap! It would take a lot to drive him insane. Once again we set about our work.

Dig, dig, dig—what a rotten job it is! The bending makes my back ache and all the blood rush to my head. Perhaps—it occurs to me later—this is accountable for the new noise that I seem to hear suddenly all round me. I could swear someone is tapping close by. I tell myself it is quite impossible that the Boches could be mining here—we are too far behind our front line. But still my ears keep echoing to that incessant, insistent thud of a pick boring steadily through soft earth. I look around the tunnel. Could that possibly be the gleam of a Boche helmet way back in the gallery? Automatically my hand reaches for the revolver on my hip. Empty! What an ass I've been! Also what an ass I'm being! If someone was mining near us, with intent to blow up our sap, surely Blackmore could hear them as well as I. And there he is digging away for dear life.

Dig, dig, dig, to the accompaniment of Weston's singing. I wish his insanity would take another turn. That inane noise is beginning to get on my nerves. I open my mouth to shout at him, and become suddenly conscious that it is dry. And there is a queer, thick feeling in my tongue. Why, of course, it was to be expected. Our fresh air is giving out! However, there is no chance now to think of it, for Weston has decided to take all our attention.

Whether my sudden movement toward him had attracted him I can't say. Anyway, he rises to his feet, and, shouting wildly, begins heaving at us handfuls of the loose earth.

"'Ere, stow that," orders Blackmore.

But the madman does not notice him. Presently, however, he desists of his own accord, and begins instead a mad gallop up and down the gallery, all the time emitting wild whoops. He stops a moment to step deliberately on our delicate instruments which crumble with a soft crash beneath his heel. We watch him help-lessly for a while, and then I decide to use authority.

"Stop that racket at once," I order, "and let us get on with our work."

His answer is a rush at me.

"Damn you," he screams. "It's all your bloody fault. You brought us here. You're burying us alive."

Well, the murder is out at last. Buried alive! A pretty prospect! But there is no time to dwell on it now. With the violence of lunacy, he starts to attack me. We clinch for a second. Then there is nothing else for it. I hit him on the head with the butt of my revolver, and he drops unconscious to the ground. Barely has he fallen when the candle goes out, leaving Blackmore and me to our efforts in the dark. We stand there baffled and helpless won-dering what on earth to do next.

"For God's sake sing or say something," I tell him irritably.

He begins to hum some old music-hall song everyone knows, but he can't keep the quaver out of his voice. The result is a sort of comical cackle.

"Lord! you're worse than the silence."

He stops at once, nothing offended. I feel a fool; also ashamed. If I am to lose heart, at least I needn't take it out on him—the staunchest and sanest pal a man could find.

We go at it again—dig, dig, dig. We keep it up for what seems hours, until my back seems broken and my brain on fire. Quite suddenly I grow sick of the whole proceeding. What's, the use of pretending any longer? We can't possibly get out by our own efforts; we can't hope to get out by anyone else's. We might just as well give in first as last—save ourselves the aching tedium of this futile digging.

"Let's ease off," I suggest to Blackmore, unwilling to confess that I'm giving in.

"Righto," comes his cheery answer. Lord! how that man can show me up!

We sit down. It must have been six in the morning. We have been at it already six hours. Weston, who has recovered consciousness, is sobbing like an ill-used child. I sense rather than see that Blackmore's head has gone down on his hands. I wonder vaguely whether he is really lost to hope, as I am, and is merely maintaining his blessed British reserve. At least thank heaven for his stoicism! It's infectious, an excellent antidote for Weston's hysteria. In silence save for the sobbing we sit there, motionless, while my eyes peer painfully through the gloom of this grave. If we could only get some light—the tiniest gleam to relieve the blackness! I realise now why the preachers paint hell as exterior darkness.

Slowly my gaze travels along the walls of the gallery. As it nears the mouth of the sap, I can scarcely repress my sudden start. For there I see a rift, tiny as the top of a tea-cup, dim and grey as the early streaks of a winter dawn. I look fixedly at it a moment. It doesn't move. It is really light! I turn my head. It is still there. I might have known—just a mirage, the trick of a tired imagination. I say nothing to Blackmore whose head is still bowed. Why worry him? He would just think that I was " seeing things." Still there it is, the size of a star. If it would only stay fixed, instead of travelling as my eye travels, round the gallery! It must be imagination. No light could pierce the walls.

It must be fifteen minutes later that Blackmore raising his head, gasps, grasps my arm, and shouts to me hoarsely:

" Light! Look! Look!"

"Where?" I ask sceptically. Let him fix its location.

"For Christ's sake are you blind?" It is his first sign of strain. "There it is at the mouth of the sap."

"Oh, yes," I answer stupidly. "Of course. so it is." Then at last the explanation dawns on me.

My eye, accustomed to the gloom, had preserved the image of this light on the retina. Everywhere I looked I saw the tiny star which was no more than a reflection still held by my optical nerve. So might your eye, reader, suddenly struck by the glare of an electric arc, keep its dazzling brilliance even after you had deflected your head. Only you, of course, would know what you were seeing. I was inclined to doubt the evidence of my own senses.

Presently we rise and grope along the gallery to investigate this new gleam of hope. Evidently when the earth crumbled in under the impact of the shell, it had failed to fill the sap completely. Just a tiny crack remained open, made perceptible by the light of day.

"Well, we won't choke to death anyway," says Blackmore very casually.

"No."

Only for this crack we might be already dead.

Once again we set to work, but there is new energy in our efforts. We keep it up for hours, never tiring but ever turning to the little light on which we depend for our life. We try to explain to Weston, but he only whimpers like a whipped child. Poor chap! Why couldn't he have held out?

I can see my watch again now. As it points to 10 a. m., the first shadow passes across the crack.

"They've come," shouts Blackmore.

We rush to the hole, and holler and holler. But evidently the damp earth retains the sound. Nothing answers us yet but the echo.

More shadows! They pass and repass repeatedly. We get impatient. How can any men be so blind?

"Good God! can't they see we're buried?" Blackmore is irritable now. We shout again, but with no better results. Shout and dig, dig and shout—this is our regular routine. With every moment our nerves are getting rawer. And then—it is 11—a sound reaches our ears. Someone digging!

"Lord! they've opened their eyes at last!"

Our own work takes on now a furious quality of energy. We dig as we never dug before. Even Weston, sensing hope, has ceased to sob at last, and has crept cautiously closer to the sap. Conversation between us has stopped absolutely, lest by any chance we should miss a welcome sound.

Twelve o'clock, and we're still here. Suppose we were mistaken after all? Suppose they are not digging toward us? Suppose they are merely clearing the trench, quite forgetting that our sap was somewhere near.

"But they must miss us—they must." Blackmore is nervous now. "I told the fellows I was coming here last night."

We shout again. No answer but the echo. Well, they're still digging. We are at least sure of that.

Twelve-thirty—we fancy we hear a voice close by. We stop to listen, but only the sound of the entrenching tool reaches us. Twelve-forty—it's coming closer. Yes, they're coming to us all right. That thud is too near for the trench. We tell Weston, but he only looks stupid and shakes his head.

One o'clock—a shaft of light shoots into the gallery. A hand comes through, then a head, then a man's whole body. I see someone bearing a lantern. I hear a voice asking a question. I try to answer, but my tongue sticks to the roof of my mouth. I throw out an arm to catch something. It is taken. The next thing I know—I am lying in the Casualty Clearing Station, with a doctor bending over my head.

"Better now?"

"Yes, thanks."

He tells me the story.

No one had missed us all evening—I hadn't said I was going to work. No one had missed us in the morning, until the Chief Royal Engineer, coming to breakfast, noticed my vacant place.

"Where is he?" he asks, being a friend of mine.

"Working in his bally sap, I suppose," said someone.

"I must drop round and tell him to hurry over before all the good things are gone." It was a Christmas breakfast, an unusually good spread.

It was about ten when, in pursuance of his thoughtful project, he dropped round to the trench and found his way blocked by a mound of earth. Quite obviously a Boche shell had pitched neatly. Immediately he set the men to work with a will. Were we alive? That was the burning question which added zest to their very earnest efforts. Yet even with their regular entrenching tools, it took them over three hours to reach us. What a chance we had had with our jack-knives and revolver!

I inquire for Blackmore. Oh! He's all right. Not a nerve seemingly in the man's whole body! Weston? Well, it seems he had been buried once before. The doctor shakes his head over the probable effects of the second shock. No wonder he had gone "potty" right away!

They send me back to my billet, where I am put to bed. Nearby is a brother officer shaving. I ask him for his mirror to gratify a sudden whim. He gives it to me, and I can scarcely believe what I see.

Can this man be I, this man with the haggard features and the hair turned so white on both sides of the head? Well, why not? Don't I feel sufficiently old and withered? I lie back, limp and lifeless, like an old man.

For two days I stay there. Then my inertia leaves me. My brain begins to cry out for new food for thought. They send me back of the line to give me a chance to recuperate. But my nerves won't leave me alone. They wake me in the night in the grip of horrid nightmares. They shake me as if with ague at the sound of sudden noise. By a desperate effort I concentrate on such work as I have to do. It relieves me somewhat, and I pluck up heart again. But nature has still a heavy toll to take for the violence done her that Christmas night.

# CHAPTER 5

# In Which the Author Repairs the Airline and Retires for Repairs Himself

1

Dumar being chosen as the most suitable health-resort for the restoration of my shaken nervous system, I was despatched there presently with a commission that called for the least possible effort on my part. Here, sixteen miles back of the line, I was out of range and out of hearing of the guns, and my billet, the cure's home, gave an added touch of peace to what was already a most peaceful setting. It was a poor home, for Catholic clergymen are not rich in French worldly goods, but the housekeeper, acting on instructions from her very hospitable master, did more than her best to make me happy. Incidentally she was Irish. How she got there I never learned, for I lacked the courage to inquire, though I confess to some curiosity on the subject. But the tea and toast she brought Lacey, my billet mate, and myself in the mornings had all the flavour of home. I never tasted the rest of her cooking, for, of course, we ate at the mess.

Lacey, a Canadian lieutenant in charge of the airline section, was my immediate superior for the time being. A very lenient superior he proved. My duties consisted in driving round each morning in a car placed entirely at my disposal, and seeing what the men were doing. In the afternoons I played football, and in the evening I prepared to sleep, the most difficult part of my work back here. I tried all the tricks enumerated by Mr. Wordsworth in his famous sonnet on the subject of insomnia, but none of them worked for me any more than for him. So for hours I would lie awake, staring straight into the dark, trying to stave off a repetition of that terrible night. Try as I would, my brain refused to rest.

With diabolical reality it reproduced one by one all the horrors I was trying to forget. Even, when, aided by an extra stiff glass of whiskey, I fell into fairly sound sleep, it was still busy, and presently it woke me. It woke me with the sound of Weston's singing ringing inanely in my ears, or the sight of Blackmore's eyes gazing despairingly into mine. At times I would find myself digging for dear life at some hard substance that refused to be moved away by my strenuous efforts. Or I would wake gasping for air and calling out that I was choking. And then realising that it was only my imagination at its old tricks, I would try to be still, while I quivered from head to foot in a perfect Turkish bath of perspiration.

Imagination can be tragically active even in retrospect. It was a very limp assistant that confronted Lacey some mornings, but fresh air can be a wonderful panacea. By degrees I slept better. Then they changed us to Vignacourt, five miles away but still back of the line. Here in the wonderful forests that make the neighbourhood famous, I found some hunting that also helped to chase the shadows. But the work itself, small as it was, proved best of all. It was my first introduction to the mysteries of the airline. Let me introduce you in turn.

## 2

The airline or overhead wiring is used to connect up telephone and telegraph instruments in positions too protected from the advent of the Boches to require any sudden or swift changes. Like the cable section, the airline consists of two detachments, each of which consists in turn of one non-commissioned officer and ten other men, one man of the ten being always mounted, usually on a bicycle. Each detachment is subdivided into two main parts. One, the front party, is responsible for the laying out of the line, the making of holes for the poles, the pre- paring of the poles and the fixing of the insulators. The other, the rear party, lays out the wire, strains and fixes it to the insulators, and erects the poles themselves.

The officer in charge of the section is usually a second lieu-tenant. His duty officially is to map out the course to be taken, but as he nearly always has two detachments working in differ-ent directions at the same time, it is quite impossible for him to act according to the letter of the law. Consequently this job often goes to the non-com. who is a sergeant.

Suppose the line is to be rigged between two villages for a distance of approximately five miles. Then No. 1, the sergeant, rides on ahead, followed at some distance by the detachment. He picks out the most suitable course to take. When possible, he avoids the main road. Cutting across country, he marks the chosen path by a trail of red flags sticking at intervals out of the earth. This done for a space of a mile or two, he returns to super-intend the work of the front party which has meantime begun, he being responsible not only for the designing but the carry-ing out of the line. He has to see, for example, that every pole is placed on the highest ground available; that it is not on the road, on a footpath or even opposite a gap in a hedge where passing traffic would be liable to knock it down. He has to see, in short, that the men don't follow the line of least resistance.

Meantime, the front party, consisting of Nos. 2, 3 and 4 have set out, accompanied by a motor lorry or horse wagon, two of which go to each detachment. On this are piled the necessary stores for the building of the line. Poles for cross-country work are fourteen feet high and about two inches in diameter; poles for crossing roads are usually eighteen feet, so as to allow for the transit underneath of traffic.

Nos. 2 and 3 of the front party carry each a sledge hammer weighing about fourteen pounds; also they have a "jumper" be-tween them. With this they "jump" the holes for the poles at intervals of eighty yards. Should a convenient tree come in their path, they fix the insulators on that, so as to save as much of their stock as possible. No. 4, who stays with the wagon, fits the holes with insulators, and passes them to the party in the rear. No. 5, who is usually a corporal, superintends the working of this rear party. No. 6 pulls a barrow on which is fitted a drum of wire, and is assisted in his task by No. 7. He, wearing a leather glove, lets the wire run off the drum through his hand, the object being to detect any possible flaws in the cable. These two, really, form an intermediary party by themselves, coming in the rear of the front and still removed from the second.

Nos. 8 and 9 wear belts to which are attached clips. Their duty consists in alternately "taking the strain." They fix the clip to the wire. Then, facing towards the rear, they bear back until the wire is as taut as possible. No. 10 comes next. He picks up the pole, fixes the wire which the straining of Nos. 8 and 9 has drawn tight, and slips it into the hold which has been jumped by Nos. 2 and 3. And so it goes at the rate of a mile and a half or perhaps two miles per hour, each man preparing the way for or supplementing the work of the other. As they approach the end of the red-flag trail, off starts the sergeant again on his pioneer work of picking up the course.

Meantime, however, the men are not left alone. For there is still No. 11, he who boasts a bicycle, continually riding up and down the whole line. His job is to keep the crew hard at their work and see that everything even to the smallest detail is properly done. Finally there is the officer, in this case occasionally myself, eternally turning up at the most unexpected moments, flying from one section to another in his swift little car. No, there is no lack of superintendents in this job, and no lack of economy in its conduct.

No object lying in the cross-country course of the detachment that is high enough to replace a pole, is ever spared. Whether it be a permanent telegraph pole already erected in the country, or a tall tree or a house-top—one and all they come in handy. And woe betide the man who fails to press them into the service as supports for his precious wire! Oh, we are terribly economical on the battle fronts of France. This, you know, is a war of materials, and the only one we must waste is human life.

### 3

My stay at Vignacourt did not last more than a month, so I was soon boosting back to my old place on the line. But it was a very stiff man who reported one evening at a Signal Office along the Somme.[1]

The chances being that my football games were over, I determined to indulge in a regular orgy at the end. In the morning I played soccer with the men—a fine bunch of athletes they were. In the afternoon I took part in a game of rugger between signal and staff officers versus the rest. It was one of those rare spectacles well worth immortalising with a movie camera, though one shrinks from the possible effects it might produce on the mind of the British public.

A civilian entering the ranks has forcibly impressed on him at various times the dignity of the High Command, the deference due to exalted station, and the disastrous consequences that follow any familiarity with his superior officers. Consider then the feelings of the raw recruit confronted by the spectacle of a general arrayed in amputated pyjamas, ducking and diving, bucking and being bucked around a second-rate football field lined most liberally by cheering Tommies! "Togs," of course, are very scarce along the front, and uniforms neither comfortable nor convenient.

So when Brigadier General T—— decided to join us in his night attire, no one expressed the least embarrassment or surprise. As he was twenty years the senior of the eldest of us, we thought, with the contempt of youth, that his presence would not add to our chances, but we were wrong. For neither his language nor his limbs had lost their vigour.

There came a stage in the game when we, the Signal and Staff, were pressing on the "Rest's" line. The brigadier was play-

---

1. *When the Somme Ran Red* by Arthur Radclyffe Dugmore also published by Leonaur.

ing scrum half-back. The burly sixteen forwards were righting for supremacy in the scrum. The old man lobbed the ball in, but instead of waiting for his forwards to heel it out, he suddenly vanished in the mass of legs. Then as suddenly out he popped on the other side, and was over the line for a try!

We were winning, with three minutes to go, and were beginning to feel ourselves safe, when a huge gunner got away down the wing. On he came like a steam engine shining with sweat, but fresh as a daisy drenched in dew. No one could stop him—we were all about in. Finally there was only me for him to pass—I was playing full back.

I had about decided that, if I could manage to bring him down, I could at least drive him into touch, but he must have guessed my intentions from my face. With a sudden swerve he turned away from the touch line to the open field. It proved to be his undoing. There came a cheer from the side-lines and a wild shout.

"Go it, pijos!" Oh! the demoralising effect of football. It was a private addressing a brigadier general!

And there came our little dynamite half-back—he was well under six feet—streaking up the field like a comet. Now he was on the big gunner who had lost ground in his attempt to swerve. Then with a yell worthy of an Indian and a string of parlour words that wouldn't have disgraced a longshoreman, he hurled him- self on his huge foe. There followed a couple of fine somersaults. Both bumped the earth. Then, as if made of rubber, up bounced our Brigadier and booted the ball down the field into touch for safety, while the gunner lay stiff and windless.

There was once a famous Dublin sportwriter who declared that, to get an angle on a game, he always sat not in the press seat but on the steps of the "Mater" hospital, where he could count the casualties from both sides as they come in. His method might have been applied nicely to our game. Swollen lips, swelled foreheads, bruised limbs, broken bones—we had them all. I got only a bloody nose, which insisted, however, on repeating its afternoon performance at intervals as I drove back that evening to my old billet.

Though a very tired man, I sat up long to hear the "latest." There were many gaps in the old ranks, some in hospital, some "gone west." There were also some promotions and decorations. In connection with the latter I must tell a story over which I confess we laughed loud and long. Incidentally it may supply psychologists with a new definition of daring. I'm afraid they have never found one to cover this case.

S—— was a friend of ours, solemn and stately, about as animated as a statue when not compelled to use his muscles. A very careful man, however, with a strict sense of his duties, but absolutely lacking in enthusiasm or inspiration.

It happened that after a very uneventful term in France he was sent home on leave of absence. He was not gone two days, when Venus accomplished what her friend, Mars, had utterly failed to perform. S——came to life with a sudden start, animated by a hopeless and helpless passion. She must have been a charmer to make this stone man melt. But alas! she was also a gay deceiver. Having raised him for a short period to the highest heavens of joy, she plunged him into the hell of despair. When he returned to the front after this disastrous encounter he had been transformed from a statue into an untamed tiger.

Cold before, he was fiery now. Where he had once been careful, he became reckless. Was there a chance of getting shot? He rushed fearlessly in. He exposed himself in and out of season. Risks were the breath of his life, for all he courted was death. There could be no doubt of it.

He wanted to get killed.

But did he? Not at all! War never takes the willing.

Instead,—so unheard of was the fortitude and enterprise he displayed—so it seemed to the uninitiated superiors—that his feats reached the ears of the general. Forthwith he was recommended for a D. S. O. He got it. Strangely enough it restored his senses. Not that he became a regular statue again, but he took the usual precautions for preserving his life. I would be willing to bet he has lost it since.

The gaps I found in the regimental ranks were not the only ones awaiting me on the line. The village, too, was poorer by one inhabitant. A very harmless and helpful creature she had always seemed, ready at any time to take on a man's laundry and turn it out for him almost "while he waited." No one had ever thought of connecting her with the mysterious accidents that had sent ammunition dumps and camouflaged batteries so often up in smoke. No one thought of it, that is, until it was proved beyond dispute.

Unusual aim on the part of the enemy guns always indicates more than average "intelligence." There are certain things, of course, which cannot be concealed from the eyes of the aviators, but dumps or dugouts are not reckoned among the number. No man can see things under the earth. Consequently, when Fritz makes an amazingly accurate hit, everyone is on the lookout for suspicious characters. But, though the town was very small, none was discovered, until an enterprising young airman got on the *qui vive*.

Looking for trouble from aloft, he allowed his eye one day to rest on some bedsheets displayed conspicuously on a lawn. White shows up well against the dark background of the earth. That is why the landing stages are painted that colour, and that is why everyone laughed at this chap, who was not much more than a novice, when he came down with his story about the old lady's laundry. She was quite old, as such people often are. It is most convenient to be able to plead senile deafness or appear doddering, when one is asked either pertinent or impertinent questions. But though his suspicions provoked sarcasm, he nevertheless received instructions not to let the said laundry out of his eye. He didn't. And one day he reported those sheets to have assumed the shape of the letter V. The next day they resembled an R. Every day they were there, weather, of course, permitting.

An investigation followed. And the boy was proved right. Those sheets were being used as semaphores to point out to enemy airmen positions worthy the attention of their guns. That is why the old lady had vanished from view, and we all had to look elsewhere for a last-minute laundress.

## 4

The brigade signal officer, having obtained a long-deferred leave, I now found myself appointed to fill his temporarily empty shoes. We spent the morning after my arrival going over the details of the job. I learned who could be trusted to do what; who showed up best in a crisis, and whose long suit was the tedium of routine. My assistants were to be sergeants, those omniscient but unobtrusive veterans who are the young subaltern's standby and best friends. When my predecessor departed for the joys of blighty that afternoon, I decided to take one of these invaluables on a tour of my sector that evening, and see for myself the lay of the land. We set out after dark, the safest time to visit the trenches. While engaged in an investigation of a certain signal dugout, we became involuntary eavesdroppers on the following conversation. Though the Leicesters[2] were manning the front line at the time, it was obvious that their ranks were not entirely composed of English blood.

"Och, the poor angashore—shure 'tis starvin' he is. Larry, give him some of your bully beef. When did they feed ye last, Jerry?"

Even if the accent had not betrayed the speaker's origin, this last would have been sufficient in itself. An Irishman, be it known, disdains the conventional Fritz when referring colloquially to his friends across No Man's Land. Unseen, I approached the opening of the dugout, and found the particular "Jerry" in question to be no more than a boy who was exhibiting an advanced stage of starvation.

"I had some black bread and three ounces of meat at twelve o'clock this morning," he announced presently in perfect English between mouthfuls.

It was now nearly twelve midnight. Evidently he had availed himself of the darkness to make his way across to our line. How

2. *1/5th Battalion the Leicestershire Regiment in the Great War* by J. D. Hills also published by Leonaur.

he had contrived to elude the sentries Heaven knows, but here he was safe and sound, a self-made and satisfied prisoner. The Irishman, however, was by no means through with his catechism. His is an enquiring and sometimes sceptical mind.

"Tell me now," he began again, when his guest had finished eating, "how came ye to desert on yer friends? Wouldn't you be better off to stay where ye were?"

"I would not," replied the German, promptly and decisively, "and if you fellows weren't so quick with your guns, there would be many glad to follow my example."

At this juncture, I thought it might be profitable to make my presence felt, so I stepped out of the surrounding shadows. Instantly the boy saw me, and stiffened to attention, after the rigid fashion of his kind. Whereupon the Irishman, pointing a finger at him, observed jocosely:

"More gun-meat we've got for you, Sir."

As he spoke, such a look of terror came into the prisoner's eyes as it is not good to see in the face of any man. With the intention of reassuring him as much as anything else, I asked him what was the matter. No one could help seeing that he was in a panic of fear.

"They told us," he said, "that if the British caught us alive, they'd shoot us, but I didn't believe it."

He had obviously taken the Irishman's remark as proof that after all "they" had been right.

"Well, why come over, if you thought there was a chance of being shot?" I asked him, after our evident amusement had allayed his fears.

"I couldn't stand it any longer," he announced. And then he told me his story

He was a Saxon, as we suspected all our opponents of being down here, and, as is well known, neither he nor any of his countrymen had much heart in the fight they are forced to make. They have no great hatred of the British, but they have much of their bosses.

"And now," he explained, "they have given us Prussian and

Bavarian officers and non-coms."

And he went on to relate how one Prussian sergeant had so ill-treated his particular chum that the chap one day lost entire control of himself and beat out his superior's brains with the butt of a gun. Naturally, he paid the penalty with his life. Which did not make things more cheerful for our young prisoner. As to how he had got across—well, he had just watched his chance, crawled over the parapet to comparative safety and then ran for bare life.

And the Saxons are not the only ones who show an unexpected affection for our side. Which leads one to wonder whether the hate fostered so sedulously by their superiors, has in reality spread very effectively through the German ranks. All along the line there have been pathetic efforts at intervals to bridge the terrible gulf that divides the fighters. On one occasion a German went so far as to stick his head over the parapet, while he shouted for such as were interested the following family information.

"I've a wife and five children in Bolton."

"Well, if ye don't put yer bloomin' 'ead down, she'll be a widdo," came the swift and uncompromising response.

Such appeals have little effect on our men's hearts. They don't curry favour, but neither do they cherish hate. Either would be too much trouble for the unemotional, lazy Britisher. War's a rotten business, but it's got to be done. Meantime let's not pretend an interest in a people who are a nuisance.

## 5

Next morning we woke to such a dim, dull day as might have provoked the illusion of being in London. Fog pressed on the window panes or streamed like smoke into the room at the slightest opening. So densely did it envelop the landscape for miles around that one might have promenaded on No Man's Land, had one desired to, without risk of interruption from the Boches. Nor was the midday sun powerful enough to dispel it.

After breakfast I repaired to the Signal Office with the gen-

115

eral intention of remaining indoors all day. But shortly after my arrival came report of a break in the cable communicating with Battalion Headquarters. As my tour of the sector had been cut short last night, I decided that here was a good opportunity to resume it with profit. So I told the lineman I would accompany him on his job. As I have intimated, dense weather is not an unmitigated disaster. Low visibility is quite desirable on the front line, allowing, as it does, a freedom of movement that would mean death on a clearer, more cheerful day. Not to be backward in taking advantage of our opportunities, we determined to ride up to the trenches.

We found the break easily enough, repaired it, tested communications and found them once more O. K. Then, with the lineman as escort, I proceeded to an investigation of the rest of the cables round here. *En route* a pile of trench revettes crossed our path. We could have got by them easily enough, but somehow I didn't want to. Instead I dismounted, giving my horse to the care of the lineman. Then I wandered off alone, leaving him sitting peaceably on the wood pile, puffing at the inevitable cigarette. What prompted me to act thus, I can't say. I simply did it without reason. People have told me Providence was protecting me, but then He was neglecting my man—which seems unfair.

Anyway about thirty feet farther on I found a line in bad condition, the insulation being eaten away. I ought to have called the lineman to mend it. Again I didn't. I don't know why. Instead I bent myself, examined it, and was beginning to patch it up, when *Bang! Crash! Stars!*

The wire faded from my vision. I fell to the earth, and lay there—I don't know really how long.

Perhaps it was an hour later, perhaps two hours, perhaps only ten minutes, when I woke to find myself still alone. I was lying on my back, with neither the force nor desire to move. All that concerned me was my head. It didn't hurt. But it felt odd, numb, heavy, as if removed from me. I put my hand up. It stuck in something prickly. That struck me as curious, but it did not disturb me. I felt my face. It was bloody. So was my coat. And where in the world was my cap? I tried to turn my head, as if to search for it. It stuck. Well, why bother? I didn't want it. I didn't want anything, unless perhaps that it might be to be left alone. I had a sort of presentiment that moving me would mean pain.

At present I had no sensation whatsoever. I was neither comfortable nor uncomfortable. It seemed almost as if I didn't exist. Here I lay, enveloped in fog, unable to see anything on any side of me. It struck me once that perhaps, if I knew it, I was dead. And then imperceptibly I slipped back into a state of coma. When I woke, I was in the Trench Dressing Station, with a bandage round my head, pressing, as it seemed to me, into my very brain.

They gave me a drink—I suppose it was some kind of spirit. Certainly it stimulated me on the spot. Sensation returned to me. Oh! how I wished it wouldn't! My head caught fire, and a hundred red-hot needles seemed to be pricking into one horrible mass of pain. Then I was seized with a rampant headache, the kind that bursts through one's eye-balls and causes one's cheeks to blaze like a flame. The more conscious I became, the worse my suffering grew. I wished to heaven I had died in the coma.

Still with consciousness came some interest in my earthly affairs. I inquired how the accident had happened. They told me that a shell had come over, hit square in the midst of the wood-pile on which my lineman was sitting so peaceably smoking his fag, had blown him and the two horses instantly to atoms, and scattered the fragments of them and the wood for yards around.

Four or five of these flying pieces had evidently caught me amidships, as I bent over the piece of worn wire. Aided by the concussion, they had thrown me forward on my head. As I fell, my hair caught in some disused barbed wire. This penetrated the scalp on the crown of my head, tearing it forward to the forehead. I rather suspected I had assisted in the tearing myself. My body must have turned as I fell. Well, I had met Indians and savages of all sorts in my travels, but it remained for the Hun to turn the old trick.

"So I've lost my scalp?" I inquired of the doctor.

"Oh, no," he reassured me. "It is simply hanging loose."

Somehow his answer gave me a sick sensation in my stomach. I started. When had I had that feeling before! When I was buried! Here I was scalped! My whole body began to tremble, and sweat to ooze from every pore. A fine chance, surely, for the old enemy to attack me! And I was right. There were many long nights ahead of me now when my head, red-hot with pain, I was to be tortured with the old torments, when imagination was to take advantage of outraged Mother Nature to conjure up abominations unknown to me before. Many a night, oppressed by that powerlessness that paralyses us in sleep, I was to try to dig with arms that refused to move, or to shout with a throat that refused to open, or to attack an enemy with a gun that refused to shoot. In the dark, before the dawn, when the vitality is lowest, and resistance at the irreducible minimum, I was to lie awake quivering with pain, confronting strange shapes and nameless horrors that faded only with the breaking of clear day.

And I am but one of many who have faced such misery. Ask any wounded soldier what is the worst part of war. He will not tell you that it is the mud or the monotony or the terrors of the hand-to-hand attack, but the nightmare after he has been restored to the normal again in a hospital back of the line. Ask any nurse what she finds hardest to bear in her work in the wards. It is not the foul smell of blood nor the filth of trench clothes nor the mangled flesh of the operating table. It is the drawn faces of the men, the haunted, harrowed look that stares at her out of their sorrowful eyes; or it is the shrill, eerie cry that wakes the ward in the night, when the man's mind reproduces the old misery in a nightmare. It is in retrospect that some soldiers suffer most. That is why death is sometimes preferable to maimed life.

6

Back in the Casualty Clearing Station one first meets women again. When I woke at C. C. S. No. 1 that evening after my jaunt in the comfortable ambulance, however, it was an orderly I found bending over my head. How that man irritated me with his benevolent, officious air! My only consolation lay in cursing him. His first duty was to shave my head. Poor chap! I suppose he went gently, but he might have been using hoop iron by the feel of it. I'd have given a good deal to use the razor on his throat. We wounded heroes give people a good deal to put up with. Gentle reader, if you are looking for a saint to canonise, search among the attendants in the Casualty Clearing Stations behind the line.

It was in the midst of his operation that a sister visited the ward. There were four of us in it, and, though she paid no attention to me, the very look of her was sufficient to soothe me. The rustle of her apron, the swish of her skirt, the sound of her voice admonishing a fellow-sufferer—they were the sweetest music I had heard in many months. And then the cool feel of her capable hand and the kind smile on her capable face! Such small things it is that restore life to the normal and help to relax the tension of trench nerves.

They kept me here a week. Then I was made ready for a move to the base. We left early one morning on what I expected would be a short trip. The towns were not more than sixty miles apart. But hour after hour passed, and still no stretcher made its appearance to take me out of the trap they call a train. At last came evening. Lo and behold we had arrived! But where? After a twelve-hour trip here we were again at Casualty Clearing Station No. 1!

"What the—!" "Why the—!"

Our language was very strong, much stronger than was warranted by the strength of our bodies.

"Did they call this a joke?" we asked one another.

But no, there was a reason. Here it is. Trains are precious things, and can't be wasted on just a few. So this one had made a tour of all the C. C. S.'s in the district picking up a burden from each. They began at the beginning which was also the end. I can only presume they thought we should like a journey. But the end was not yet. Though it was late in the evening, the train could not be halted on its trip. So off we set again, this time really for the base which, as I remember, was General Hospital No. 3.

Here I had hoped to make but a call *en route* for "Blighty" and home. But again I was fated to be disappointed. In all, my stay consisted of about six weeks. They refused to trust me before that to the Channel. Bandaging twice a day broke what might have been monotony. Headaches and the smell of a drug kept me quiescent, if not amused. I learned to distinguish between sisters. There were many of them here, some of the variety which is known to the Tommy as the "Niggle-Naggles," a very apt name. These were the ladies who administered your medicine, adjusted your pillows and pointed out your sins with the air of a teacher addressing a naughty class. Efficient, omniscient, industrious creatures, they are fortunately rare. For if there is one thing needed in a war nurse, it is a quality of humanity. Most of them possessed it. Bless their souls!

The doctor, a genial creature, had no small load on his hands. Possibly the heaviest item in his burden was a Boche officer who was not far from me. He was a Prussian, and like most of his kind, spoke very passable English. Some of our chaps who could walk, tried visiting him at first. This is customary. We know the captives are lonely. But they met with a cool reception, so they stopped pretty soon. They thought he didn't understand what they were saying. The doctor, however, knew better. Trying to diagnose the blighter's trouble, which was internal, he put him a couple of questions about his wound.

"That's your business to find out," was the very amiable answer. After this snap, he relapsed into silence.

If I had been the doctor, I'd have been tempted to let him die.

Came the news that a convoy was crossing! We have been hearing that at intervals for weeks, and each time it has raised hopes destined to be disappointed. But my turn has come at last. For ten days I have been allowed to roam the corridors, with short little spells of walking in the open. Now I am declared fit to be sent home. An orderly has already packed my belongings.

They are even now preceding me to the Dieppe boat. I am to follow them in the morning.

It is a glorious day, though the snow is thick on the ground, clogging the wheels of our slow-moving ambulance.

"'E 1' out first!"

That means me, among others. I am able to walk aboard alone. Following us is a long line of sitting cases and stretcher cases. These latter are put to bed straight away. We can roam on deck, if we so choose. God! It's a great thing to be alive after all, and fill your lungs with salt sea air!

Dover! We're across! Our landing is made quietly. Right up to the pier runs the train to take us to London. We're dog-tired. The excitement is too much after the monotony. We slouch in our seats, and try to read the home news. Presently comes Captain Bland with his bunch of tickets. He takes our names, and hands us a slip.

"King's College all right for you?"

"No more dangerous than the rest?"

He laughs. We're all in great humour.

And then Charing Cross and its cheering crowds! Nurses come to collect us for our various hospitals. They put us in luxurious cars lent by private owners. Our laps are laden with flowers hurled at us through open windows.

Presently my head begins to reel. A mist comes before my eyes, but my brain is fairly clear.

"You're all right," I tell myself. "You're home. What more do you want?"

I slip back semi-unconscious among a pile of receding cushions, secure in this new sense of complete safety.

LEONAUR

# ALSO FROM LEONAUR
## AVAILABLE IN SOFTCOVER OR HARDCOVER WITH DUST JACKET

**FARAWAY CAMPAIGN** *by F. James*—Experiences of an Indian Army Cavalry Officer in Persia & Russia During the Great War.

**REVOLT IN THE DESERT** *by T. E. Lawrence*—An account of the experiences of one remarkable British officer's war from his own perspective.

**MACHINE-GUN SQUADRON** *by A. M. G.*—The 20th Machine Gunners from British Yeomanry Regiments in the Middle East Campaign of the First World War.

**A GUNNER'S CRUSADE** *by Antony Bluett*—The Campaign in the Desert, Palestine & Syria as Experienced by the Honourable Artillery Company During the Great War .

**DESPATCH RIDER** *by W. H. L. Watson*—The Experiences of a British Army Motorcycle Despatch Rider During the Opening Battles of the Great War in Europe.

**TIGERS ALONG THE TIGRIS** *by E. J. Thompson*—The Leicestershire Regiment in Mesopotamia During the First World War.

**HEARTS & DRAGONS** *by Charles R. M. F. Crutwell*—The 4th Royal Berkshire Regiment in France and Italy During the Great War, 1914-1918.

**INFANTRY BRIGADE: 1914** *by John Ward*—The Diary of a Commander of the 15th Infantry Brigade, 5th Division, British Army, During the Retreat from Mons.

**DOING OUR 'BIT'** *by Ian Hay*—Two Classic Accounts of the Men of Kitchener's 'New Army' During the Great War including *The First 100,000 & All In It.*

**AN EYE IN THE STORM** *by Arthur Ruhl*—An American War Correspondent's Experiences of the First World War from the Western Front to Gallipoli-and Beyond.

**STAND & FALL** *by Joe Cassells*—With the Middlesex Regiment Against the Bolsheviks 1918-19.

**RIFLEMAN MACGILL'S WAR** *by Patrick MacGill*—A Soldier of the London Irish During the Great War in Europe including *The Amateur Army, The Red Horizon & The Great Push.*

**WITH THE GUNS** *by C. A. Rose & Hugh Dalton*—Two First Hand Accounts of British Gunners at War in Europe During World War 1- Three Years in France with the Guns and With the British Guns in Italy.

**THE BUSH WAR DOCTOR** *by Robert V. Dolbey*—The Experiences of a British Army Doctor During the East African Campaign of the First World War.

LEONAUR

# ALSO FROM LEONAUR

## AVAILABLE IN SOFTCOVER OR HARDCOVER WITH DUST JACKET

**WINGED WARFARE** *by William A. Bishop*—The Experiences of a Canadian 'Ace' of the R.F.C. During the First World War.

**THE STORY OF THE LAFAYETTE ESCADRILLE** *by George Thenault*—A famous fighter squadron in the First World War by its commander..

**R.F.C.H.Q.** *by Maurice Baring*—The command & organisation of the British Air Force during the First World War in Europe.

**SIXTY SQUADRON R.A.F.** *by A. J. L. Scott*—On the Western Front During the First World War.

**THE STRUGGLE IN THE AIR** *by Charles C. Turner*—The Air War Over Europe During the First World War.

**WITH THE FLYING SQUADRON** *by H. Rosher*—Letters of a Pilot of the Royal Naval Air Service During the First World War.

**OVER THE WEST FRONT** *by "Spin" & "Contact'* —Two Accounts of British Pilots During the First World War in Europe, Short Flights With the Cloud Cavalry by "Spin" and Cavalry of the Clouds by "Contact".

**SKYFIGHTERS OF FRANCE** *by Henry Farré*—An account of the French War in the Air during the First World War.

**THE HIGH ACES** *by Laurence la Tourette Driggs*—French, American, British, Italian & Belgian pilots of the First World War 1914-18.

**PLANE TALES OF THE SKIES** *by Wilfred Theodore Blake*—The experiences of pilots over the Western Front during the Great War.

**IN THE CLOUDS ABOVE BAGHDAD** *by J. E. Tennant*—Recollections of the R. F. C. in Mesopotamia during the First World War against the Turks.

**THE SPIDER WEB** *by P. I. X. (Theodore Douglas Hallam)*—Royal Navy Air Service Flying Boat Operations During the First World War by a Flight Commander

**EAGLES OVER THE TRENCHES** *by James R. McConnell & William B. Perry*—Two First Hand Accounts of the American Escadrille at War in the Air During World War 1-Flying For France: With the American Escadrille at Verdun and Our Pilots in the Air

**KNIGHTS OF THE AIR** *by Bennett A. Molter*—An American Pilot's View of the Aerial War of the French Squadrons During the First World War.

LEONAUR

# ALSO FROM LEONAUR
## AVAILABLE IN SOFTCOVER OR HARDCOVER WITH DUST JACKET

**AN APACHE CAMPAIGN IN THE SIERRA MADRE** *by John G. Bourke*—An Account of the Expedition in Pursuit of the Chiricahua Apaches in Arizona, 1883.

**BILLY DIXON & ADOBE WALLS** *by Billy Dixon and Edward Campbell Little*—Scout, Plainsman & Buffalo Hunter, *Life and Adventures of "Billy" Dixon* by Billy Dixon and *The Battle of Adobe Walls* by Edward Campbell Little (*Pearson's Magazine*).

**WITH THE CALIFORNIA COLUMN** *by George H. Petis*—Against Confederates and Hostile Indians During the American Civil War on the South Western Frontier, *The California Column, Frontier Service During the Rebellion* and *Kit Carson's Fight With the Comanche and Kiowa Indians.*

**THRILLING DAYS IN ARMY LIFE** *by George Alexander Forsyth*—Experiences of the Beecher's Island Battle 1868, the Apache Campaign of 1882, and the American Civil War.

**INDIAN FIGHTS AND FIGHTERS** *by Cyrus Townsend Brady*—Indian Fights and Fighters of the American Western Frontier of the 19th Century.

**THE NEZ PERCÉ CAMPAIGN, 1877** *by G. O. Shields & Edmond Stephen Meany*—Two Accounts of Chief Joseph and the Defeat of the Nez Percé, *The Battle of Big Hole* by G. O. Shields and *Chief Joseph, the Nez Percé* by Edmond Stephen Meany.

**CAPTAIN JEFF OF THE TEXAS RANGERS** *by W. J. Maltby*—Fighting Comanche & Kiowa Indians on the South Western Frontier 1863-1874.

**SHERIDAN'S TROOPERS ON THE BORDERS** *by De Benneville Randolph Keim*—The Winter Campaign of the U. S. Army Against the Indian Tribes of the Southern Plains, 1868-9.

**WILD LIFE IN THE FAR WEST** *by James Hobbs*—The Adventures of a Hunter, Trapper, Guide, Prospector and Soldier.

**THE OLD SANTA FE TRAIL** *by Henry Inman*—The Story of a Great Highway.

**LIFE IN THE FAR WEST** *by George F. Ruxton*—The Experiences of a British Officer in America and Mexico During the 1840's.

**ADVENTURES IN MEXICO AND THE ROCKY MOUNTAINS** *by George F. Ruxton*—Experiences of Mexico and the South West During the 1840's.

LEONAUR

# ALSO FROM LEONAUR
### AVAILABLE IN SOFTCOVER OR HARDCOVER WITH DUST JACKET

**THE ART OF WAR** *by Antoine Henri Jomini*—Strategy & Tactics From the Age of Horse & Musket.

**THE ART OF WAR** *by Sun Tzu and Pierre G. T. Beauregard*—*The Art of War* by Sun Tzu and *Principles and Maxims of the Art of War* by Pierre G. T. Beauregard.

**THE MILITARY RELIGIOUS ORDERS OF THE MIDDLE AGES** *by F. C. Woodhouse*—The Knights Templar, Hospitaller and Others.

**THE BENGAL NATIVE ARMY** *by F. G. Cardew*—An Invaluable Reference Resource.

**ARTILLERY THROUGH THE AGES**—*by Albert Manucy*—A History of the DEvelopment and Use of Cannons, Mortars, Rockets & Projectiles from Earliest Times to the Nineteenth Century.

**THE SWORD OF THE CROWN** *by Eric W. Sheppard*—A History of the British Army to 1914.

**THE 7TH (QUEEN'S OWN) HUSSARS: Volume 3—1818-1914** *by C. R. B. Barrett*—On Campaign During the Canadian Rebellion, the Indian Mutiny, the Sudan, Matabeleland, Mashonaland and the Boer War Volume 3: 1818-1914.

**THE CAMPAIGN OF WATERLOO** *by Antoine Henri Jomini*—A Political & Military History from the French perspective.

**THE AUXILIA** OF THE ROMAN IMPERIAL ARMY *by G. L. Cheeseman.*

**RIFLE & DRILL** *by S. Bertram Browne*—The Enfield Rifle Musket, 1853 and the Drill of the British Soldier of the Mid-Victorian Period *A Companion to the New Rifle Musket* and *A Practical Guide to Squad and Setting-up Dtill.*

**NAPOLEON'S MEN AND METHODS** *by Alexander L. Kielland*—The Rise and Fall of the Emperor and His Men Who Fought by His Side.

**THE WOMAN IN BATTLE** *by Loreta Janeta Velazquez*—Soldier, Spy and Secret Service Agent for the Confederancy During the American Civil War.

**THE MILITARY SYSTEM OF THE ROMANS** *by Albert Harkness.*

**THE BATTLE OF ORISKANY 1777** *by Ellis H. Roberts*—The Conflict for the Mowhawk Valley During the American War of Independenc.

**PERSONAL RECOLLECTIONS OF JOAN OF ARC** *by Mark Twain.*